CHINESE

in 10 minutes a day®

by **Kristine Kershul**, M.A., University of California, Santa Barbara

adapted by **Wáng Yǐn Zhēn**

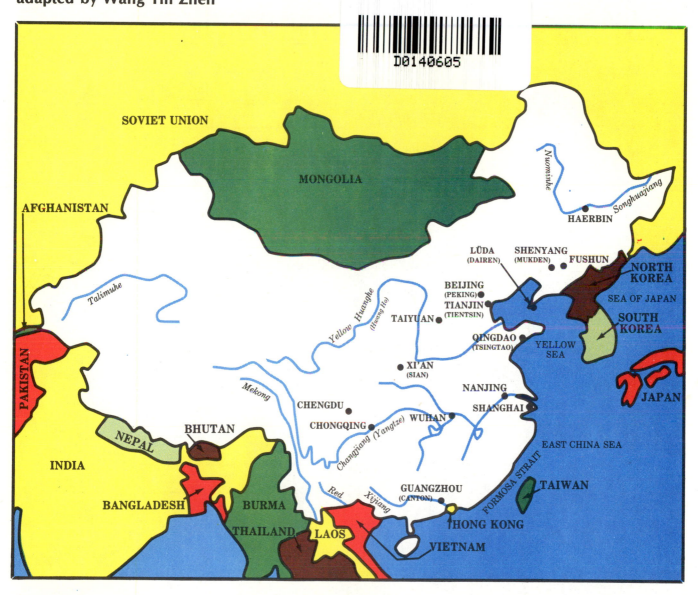

Published by
Bilingual Books, Inc.
6018 Seaview Avenue N.W.
Seattle, Washington 98107
Telephone: (206) 789-7544
Telex: 499 6629 BBKS UI

Distributed by
USA: Cliffs Notes, Box 80728, Lincoln, Nebraska 68501
UK: Ruskin Book Services, 15 Comberton Hill, Kidderminster, Worcestershire DY10 1QG

(peen-yeen)
Pīnyīn
tool

Pīnyīn is a tool to help people read Chinese easily. To learn the Chinese sound of these letters, write each example in the space provided.

Pīnyīn	English sound	Example	(Write it here)	Meaning
a	ah	chāzi *(chah-zuh)*	*chāzi*	fork
ai	i/y	Shànghǎi *(shahng-hi)*		Shanghai
ao	ow	hǎo *(how)*		good
c	ts *(as in its)*	cǎo *(tsow)*		grass
e	uh	hē *(huh)*		to drink
e	eh *(after y,u,i)*	yè *(yeh)*		night
ei	a/ay	Běijīng *(bay-jeeng)*		Peking
i	ee	nǐ *(nee)*		you
i	r *(after c,ch,s,sh,z,zh)*	chī *(chr)*		to eat
ia	ee-ah	jiā *(jee-ah)*		home
iu	yoo	qiú *(chee-yoo)*		ball
o	wo	pǒ *(pwo)*		slope
ou	oh	hòu *(hoh)*	*hòu*	thick
q	ch	qīng *(cheeng)*		clear
u	oo	shū *(shoo)*		book
ü	yew	yú *(yew)*		fish
ua	wah	shuāzi *(shwah-zuh)*		brush
uai	wy	kuàizi *(kwy-zuh)*		chopstick(s)
ue	yoo-eh	yùe *(yoo-eh)*		month
ui	wee	shùi *(shwee)*		to sleep
un	oon	yún *(yoon)*		cloud
uo	woh	shǔo *(shwoh)*		to speak
x	ss	xīn *(sseen)*		new
zi	zuh	zì *(zuh)*		word(s)
zh	juh	Zhōngguó *(jung-gwoh)*		China

Chinese is a tonal language with four basic tones.
1. The voice produces a flat, high pitch (—).
2. The voice rises from middle pitch to high pitch (/).
3. The voice drops from middle pitch to low pitch and then rises to high pitch (∨).
4. The voice falls from high pitch to low pitch (\).

2

When you arrive in **Běijīng,** *(bay-jeeng)* / Peking, the very first thing you will need to do is to ask questions — "Where is the train station?" "Where can I exchange money?" "Where *(nahr)* **(nǎr)** is the lavatory?" "**Nǎr** *(nahr)* / where is a restaurant?" "**Nǎr** do I catch a taxi?" "**Nǎr** is a good hotel?" "**Nǎr** is my luggage?" — and the list will go on and on for the entire length of your visit. In Chinese, there are NINE KEY QUESTION WORDS to learn. With these nine **zì,** *(zuh)* / words you can ask questions correctly. They will help you find out what you are ordering in a restaurant before you order it and not after the surprise (or shock!) arrives. These **zì** *(zuh)* / words are extremely important, so learn them now.

Take a few minutes to study and practice saying the nine question **zì** *(zuh)* listed below. Then cover the **zì** *(zuh)* with your hand and fill in each of the blanks with the matching Chinese **zì.** *(zuh)* / word

1.	**NǍR** *(nahr)*	=	WHERE	_____
2.	**SHÉNME** *(shun-muh)*	=	WHAT	_____
3.	**SHEI** *(shay)*	=	WHO	*shéi, shéi, shéi*
4.	**WĚISHÉNME** *(way-shun-muh)*	=	WHY	_____
5.	**SHÉNME SHÍHÒU** *(shun-muh)* *(shr-hoh)*	=	WHEN	_____
6.	**ZĚNME** *(zuhn-muh)*	=	HOW	_____
7.	**DŌUSHǍO** *(dwoh-show)*	=	HOW MUCH / HOW MANY	_____
8.	**JǏ** *(jee)*	=	HOW MANY	_____
9.	**NEI (NǍ)** *(nay)* *(nah)*	=	WHICH	_____

Now test yourself to see if you really can keep these *(zuh)* **zì** straight in your mind. Draw lines

between the *(jung-gwoh)* **Zhōngguó** *(zuh)* **zì** and their English equivalents below.
Chinese · words

(nahr)
nǎr — who

(nay) (nah)
nei (na) — how many

(shun-muh)
shénme — where

(shay)
shei — why

(way-shun-muh)
wèishénme — how

(shun-muh) (shr-hoh)
shénme shíhòu — what

(zuh-mu)
zěnme — which

(dwoh-show)
dūoshǎo — how much

(jee)
jǐ — when

Examine the following questions containing these **zì**. Practice the sentences out loud and

then quiz yourself by filling in the blanks below with the correct question **zì**.

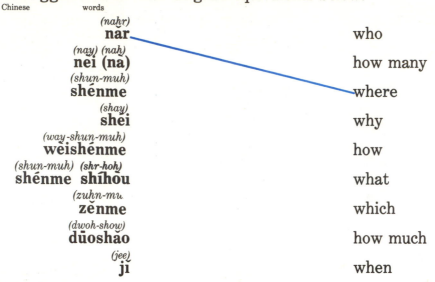

(dee-ahn-hwah) (zi) (nahr)
Dìanhùa zai nǎr? 电话
Telephone is where?

(nah) (shr) (shay)
Na shi shei?
That is who?

(hwoh-chuh) (shun-muh) (shr-hoh)
Hǔochē shénme shíhou
(li)
lái? 火车
Train what time comes?

(juh) (guh)(dwoh-show) (chee-ahn)
Zhè ge dūoshǎo qian?
This how much money?

(zuhn-muh) (luh)
Zěnme le?
How is wrong?

(sah-lah)(zuhn-muh)(yahng)
Sālà zěnme yàng?
Salad how is?

(nah) (guh)(nahn-ruhn)(shun-muh) (shr-hoh) (li)
Nà gè nánrén shénme shíhòu lái?
That man what time comes?

(way-shun-muh) (hwoh-chuh) (boo) (li)
Wèishénme hǔochē bù lái?
Why train not come?

(dee-ahn-hwah) (zi)
1. **Dìanhùa zài** _____ ?

(nah) (shr)
2. **Nà shi** _____ ?

(hwoh-chuh)   *(li)*
3. **Hǔochē** *shénme shíhòu* **lái?**

(juh) (guh)   *(chee-ahn)*
4. **Zhè gè** _____ **qian?**

(luh)
5. _____ **le?**

(sah-lah)   *(yahng)*
6. **Sālà** _____ **yàng?**

(nah) (guh) (nahn-ruhn)   *(li)*
7. **Nà gè nánrén** _____ **lái?**

(hwoh-chuh) (boo) (li)
8. _____ **hǔochē bù lái?**

(nahr)
Nǎr will be your most used question **zì**, so let's concentrate on it. Say each of the

following *(jung-gwoh)* **Zhōngguó** sentences aloud. Then write out each sentence without looking at the
Chinese

example. If you don't succeed on the first try, don't give up. Just practice each sentence

until you are able to do it easily.

Don't forget that you pronounce **"ai"** like "eye" and **"ia"** like "ee-ah." Also use your

(peen-yeen)
4 pīnyīn when new **zì** are introduced.

(nahr) (yoh) (tsuh-swoh)
Năr yǒu cèsuǒ?
where is lavatory 厕所

MEN / WOMEN

(nahr) (yoh) (choo-zoo-chuh)
Năr yǒu chūzuchē?
where is taxi
出租车

(yoh) (goong-goong-chee-chuh)
Năr yǒu gōnggòngqìchē?
(public) bus 公共汽车

(fahn-gwar)
Năr yǒu fàngŭar?
restaurant 饭馆

(yeen-hahng)
Năr yǒu yínháng?
bank 银行

(lew-gwahn)
Năr yǒu lüǧuǎn?
hotel 旅馆

Chinese and English are obviously very different languages, but some things are easier to say in Chinese. Notice how similar questions and statements are in Chinese.

(nahr) (yoh) (tsuh-swoh)
Năr yǒu cèsuo? (question)

(juhr)
Zhèr yǒu cèsǔo. (statement)
here

(shun-muh)
Shénme is also a very useful question **zì**. From **shénme**, you can make other question
what

word combinations. Let's learn them now.

shénme *(shr-hoh)* **shíhòu** = when   **shénme** *(dee-fahng)* **dìfāng** = what place (where)   **shénme** *(ruhn)* **rèn** = what person (who)

Below are more **zì** for you to learn as you work your way through this *(shoo)* **shū.**
book

Gradually practice using the **Zhōnggúo** tones (review page 2) with these new **zì**.
- ☑ **chāzi** *(chah-zuh)* . . . . fork   *chāzi*
- ☑ **chízi** *(chee-zuh)* . . . . spoon
- ☑ **dāozi** *(dow-zuh)* . . . . knife
- ☑ **kùaizi** *(kwy-zuh)* . . . . chopsticks

筷子
kuaizi

Additional fun **zì** will appear at the bottom of the following pages in a yellow color band.

Be sure to say each **zì** aloud and then write out the *(jung-gwoh)* **Zhōnggúo zì** in the blank to the right.
Chinese

5

Step 2

zhè and nǎ
(juh) *(nah)*

Zhōngguó hùa *(hwah)* language does not have **zì** for "the" and "a." Instead **zhè** *(juh)* and **nà** *(nah)* are used.

zhè *(juh)* = this or these   **nà** *(nah)* = that or those

In **Zhōngguó hùa, zhè** *(juh)* and **nà** *(nah)* reflect the article's distance from the speaker.

zhè shū *(juh) (shoo)*
this   book   vs.   **nà shū**
that book

zhè jī *(jee)*
chicken   vs.   **nà jī**

zhè yú *(juh) (yew)*
fish   vs.   **nà yú**

zhè dìanhùa *(dee-ahn-hwah)*
telephone   vs.   **nà dìanhùa**

In addition to **zhè** *(juh)* and **nà,** *(nah)* Chinese has "measure words" for everything. These are generally numbers like "one" room or quantities like "piece" of paper. **Běn** *(buhn)* is an example of a Chinese measure **zì. Běn,** *(buhn)* meaning "bound together," is used with words like book and magazine.

yì běn shū *(yee) (buhn) (shoo)*
one bound book

yì běn zázhì *(yee) (buhn) (zah-juhr)*
one bound magazine

Oftentimes, Chinese "measure words" can not be translated into English. These measure words will be marked (M).

Step 3

dōngxi *(dwong-ssee)*
things

Before you proceed with this step, situate yourself comfortably in your living room. Now look around you. Can you name the things which you see in this **wūzi** *(woo-zuh)* room in Chinese? You can probably guess **shāfā** *(shah-fah)* means sofa, but let's learn the rest of them. After practicing these **zì** out loud, write them in the blanks below and on the next page.

hùar *(hwar)* = the picture _____*hùar*_____

tīanhūabǎn *(tee-yahn-hwah-bahn)* = the ceiling _____

☐ **chē** *(chuh)* .... vehicle
☐ **chēfū** *(chuh-foo)* .... driver
☐ **chēlún** *(chun-loon)* .... wheel   车
☐ **chēfáng** *(chuh-fahng)* .... garage   *che*
6 ☐ **chēzhàn** *(chuh-jahn)* .... bus stop

(chee-ahng-jee-ow)
qiángjiǎo = (the) corner _____

(chwahng-hoo)
chuānghù = (the) window _____

(dung)
dēng = (the) light _____

(ti-dung)
táidēng = (the) lamp _____

(shah-fah)
shāfā = (the) sofa _____

(yee-zuh)
yǐzi = (the) chair _____

(dee-tahn)
dìtǎn = (the) carpet _____

(jwoh-zuh)
zhuōzi = (the) table _____

(muhn)
mén = (the) door _____

(jung)
zhōng = (the) clock _____

(chwahng-lee-ahn)
chuānglián = (the) curtain *chuānglián*

(chee-ahng)
qiáng = (the) wall _____

Remember that **Zhōngguó hùa** *(hwah)* has no "the." Use **zhè** *(juh)* or **nà** *(nah)* before the object to indicate
language   this   that
something in particular or use a number. Even easier, don't use anything at all. Now open

your **shū** *(shoo)* to the first page with the stick-on labels. Peel off the first 14 labels and
book

proceed around the room, labeling these items in your **jiā** *(jee-ah)*. This will help to increase your
home

Zhōngguó zì power easily. Do not forget to say the **zì** as you attach each label.

Now ask yourself, "**Shāfā** *(shah-fah)* **zài** *(zi)* **nǎr** *(nahr)*?" and point at it while you answer "**Shāfā** *(shah-fah)* **zài** *(zi)* **zhèr** *(juhr)*."
sofa   is   where   sofa   is

Continue on down the list until you feel comfortable with these **xīn zì** *(sseen)*. Say, "**Shū**
new   book

zài *(zi)* **nǎr**?" Then reply, "**Shū zài zhèr** *(juhr)*," and so on. When you can identify all the **dōngxi** *(dwong-ssee)*
things

on the list, you will be ready to move on.

Now, starting on the next page, let's learn some basic parts of the house.

☐ **diànchē** *(dee-ahn-chuh)* .... trolley _____
☐ **huǒchē** *(hwoh-chuh)* .... train _____
☐ **qìchē** *(chee-chuh)* .... car _____
☐ **sānlúnchē** *(sahn-loon-chuh)* .... pedicab 车 _____
☐ **zìxíngchē** *(zuh-sseeng-chuh)* .... bicycle *che* _____

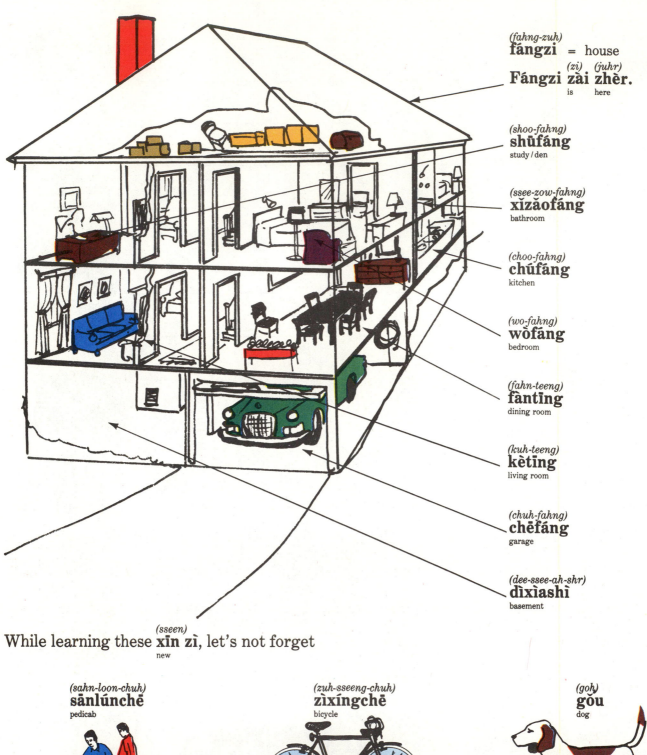

(fahng-zuh)
fángzi = house

(zi) *(juhr)*
Fángzi zài zhèr.
is   here

(shoo-fahng)
shūfáng
study / den

(ssee-zow-fahng)
xǐzǎofáng
bathroom

(choo-fahng)
chúfáng
kitchen

(wo-fahng)
wòfáng
bedroom

(fahn-teeng)
fàntīng
dining room

(kuh-teeng)
kètīng
living room

(chuh-fahng)
chēfáng
garage

(dee-ssee-ah-shr)
dìxiàshì
basement

(sseen)
While learning these **xīn zì**, let's not forget
new

(sahn-loon-chuh)
sānlúnchē
pedicab

(zuh-sseeng-chuh)
zìxíngchē
bicycle

(goh)
gǒu
dog

sānlúnchē

_____   _____

(mow)
māo
cat

(hwah-yoo-ahn)
hūayúan
garden

(sseen)
xìn
letters

xìn

(yoh-twong)
youtǒng
mailbox

(hwar)
hūar (**hùar** means picture)
flowers

(muhn-leeng)
ménlíng
doorbell

Peel off the next set of labels and wander through your *(fahng-zuh)* **fángzi** learning these *(sseen)* **xīn** *(zuh)* **zì**.
house / new / words

Granted, it will be somewhat difficult to label your *(goh)* **gǒu**, *(mow)* **māo** or *(hwar)* **hūar**, but use your

imagination.

Again, practice by asking yourself, "*(hwah-yoo-ahn)(zi)* **Hūayúan zài** *(nahr)* **nǎr?**" or "**Nǎr** *(yoh)* **yǒu** *(hwah-yoo-ahn)* **hūayúan?**"
is / where / where / is

and reply, "**Hūayúan zài zhěr.**"
(juhr)
here

(nahr) *(yoh)*
Nǎr yǒu
where is

☐ **fěnbǐ** *(fuhn-bee)*	chalk	笔
☐ **gāngbǐ** *(gahng-bee)*	pen	
☐ **máobǐ** *(mow-bee)*	writing brush	*bǐ*
☐ **qianbǐ** *(chee-ahn-bee)*	pencil	
☐ **yúanzǐbǐ** *(yoo-ahn-zuh-bee)*	ballpoint pen	

Step 4

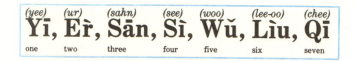

(yee)	*(ur)*	*(sahn)*	*(see)*	*(woo)*	*(lee-oo)*	*(chee)*
Yī,	**Èr,**	**Sān,**	**Sì,**	**Wǔ,**	**Lìu,**	**Qī**
one	two	three	four	five	six	seven

(yee) **yī,** **yī,** *(ur)* **yī** **èr,** **èr** **yī,** **yī** **èr** *(sahn)* **sān,** **sān** **èr** **yī,**
one   two   three

(see) *(woo)* *(lee-oo)* *(chee)* **yī** **èr** **sān** **sì** **wǔ** **lìu** **qī.**
four five six seven

In **Zhōngguó,** *(jung-gwoh)* / China, as in America, children choose sides for games by reciting a counting rhyme like the one above. In other ways, however, **shùzì** *(shoo-zuh)* / numbers are used differently in the **Zhōngguó hùa** *(hwah)* / language. Unlike English, in **Zhōngguó hùa,** days and months are indicated by **shùzì** *(shoo-zuh)* / number.

For example, **yī** **yùe** *(yee) (yoo-eh)* / month, meaning one or first month, means January in **Zhōngguó hùa.**

When learning the following **shùzì** *(shoo-zuh)*, notice the similarities (underlined) between numbers like **èr** *(ur)* (2) and **shíèr** *(shr-ur)* (12), and **qī** *(chee)* (7) and **shíqī** *(shr-chee)* (17). After practicing the **shùzì** out loud, cover the **Zhōngguó zì** and write out the **shùzì** 1 through 10 in the blanks.
numbers

0	*(leeng)* **líng**			**0**	*líng*
1	*(yee)* **yī**	**11**	*(shr-yee)* **shíyī**	**1**	_____
2	*(ur)* **èr**	**12**	*(shr-ur)* **shíer**	**2**	_____
3	*(sahn)* **sān**	**13**	*(shr-sahn)* **shísān**	**3**	_____
4	*(see)* **sì**	**14**	*(shr-see)* **shísì**	**4**	_____
5	*(woo)* **wǔ**	**15**	*(shr-woo)* **shíwǔ**	**5**	_____
6	*(lee-oo)* **lìu**	**16**	*(shr-lee-oo)* **shílìu**	**6**	_____
7	*(chee)* **qī**	**17**	*(shr-chee)* **shíqī**	**7**	_____
8	*(bah)* **bā**	**18**	*(shr-bah)* **shíbā**	**8**	_____
9	*(jee-oo)* **jǐu**	**19**	*(shr-jee-oo)* **shíjǐu**	**9**	_____
10	*(shr)* **shí**	**20**	*(ur-shr)* **èrshí**	**10**	_____

☐ **dìan** *(dee-ahn)* . . . . electricity
☐ **dìanbāng** *(dee-ahn-bahng)* . . . . flashlight
☐ **dìanbào** *(dee-ahn-bow)* . . . . telegram
☐ **dìanhùa** *(dee-ahn-hwah)* . . . . telephone
☐ **dìannǎo** *(dee-ahn-now)* . . . . computer

電
dian

_____
_____
_____
_____

Use these **shùzì** on a daily basis. Count to yourself in **Zhōnggúo hùa** when you brush your teeth, exercise, or commute to work. Now fill in the following blanks according to the **shùzì** given in the parentheses.

Note: This is a good time to start learning these two important phrases.

(woh) (ssee-ahng) (yow)
wǒ xiǎng   yào   =   I would like   _____

(woh-muhn) (ssee-ahng) (yow)
wǒmén xiǎng   yào   =   we would like   _____

(woh) (ssee-ahng) (yow) **Wǒ xiǎng yào** _____ (15)	*(jahng) (juhr)* **zhǎng zhǐ.** sheets paper	*(dwoh-show)* **Dūoshǎo?** how much _____ (15)
Wǒ xiǎng yào _____ (10)	*(meeng-sseen-pee-ahn)* **zhǎng míngxìnpìan.** (M) postcards 明信片	*(dwoh-show)* **Dūoshǎo?** _____ (10)
Wǒ xiǎng yào _____ (11)	*(yoh-pee-ow)* **zhǎng yóupìao.** (M) stamps 邮票	**Dūoshǎo?** _____ (11)
Wǒ xiǎng yào _*bā*_ (8)	*(jee-ah-loon) (chee-yoh)* **jīalún qìyóu.** gallons gasoline	**Dūoshǎo?** _____ (8)
Wǒ xiǎng yào _____ (1)	*(bay) (joo-zuh-shwee)* **běi júzishǔi.** cup orange juice	**Dūoshǎo?** _____ (1)
(woh-muhn) (ssee-ahng) (yow) **Wǒmén xiǎng yào** _____ (3)	*(jahng) (ssee-pee-ow)* **zhǎng xìpiao.** theater tickets	**Dūoshǎo?** _____ (3)
Wǒmén xiǎng yào _____ (4)	*(bay) (chah)* **běi chá.** cup tea 茶	**Dūoshǎo?** _____ (4)
Wǒmén xiǎng yào _____ (2)	*(bay) (pee-jee-oo)* **běi píjǐu.** glass beer	**Dūoshǎo?** _____ (2)
Wǒmén xiǎng yào _____ (12)	*(guh)(sseen-ssee-ahn)(jee-dahn)* **gè xīnxian jīdàn.** (M) fresh eggs	**Dūoshǎo?** _____ (12)
Wǒmén xiǎng yào _____ (6)	*(bahng) (roh)* **bàng ròu.** pounds meat	**Dūoshǎo?** _____ (6)
Wǒmén xiǎng yào _____ (5)	*(bay) (shwee)* **běi shǔi.** water	**Dūoshǎo?** _____ (5)
Wǒmén xiǎng yào _____ (7)	*(jee-oo)* **bēi jǐu.** wine 酒	**Dūoshǎo?** _*qī*_ (7)
Wǒmén xiǎng yào _____ (9)	*(bahng) (hwahng-yoh)* **bàng húangyóu.** (M) butter	**Dūoshǎo?** _____ (9)

☐ **dìanshì** *(dee-ahn-shr)* . . . . television   _____
☐ **dìantái** *(dee-ahn-ti)* . . . . radio station   _____
☐ **dìantī** *(dee-ahn-tee)* . . . . elevator   **电**   _____
☐ **dìanyǐng** *(dee-ahn-yeeng)* . . . . movie   *dian*   _____
☐ **dìanzhōng** *(dee-ahn-jung)* . . . . electric clock   _____

11

In **Zhōngwén, liǎng** *(lee-ahng)* also means two.

Now see if you can translate the following thoughts into **Zhōngwén** *(jung-wuhn)*. Chinese language The answers are at the bottom of **zhě** *(juh)* **yè** *(yeh)*.
this   page

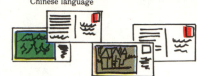

1. I would like seven postcards.

_____

2. I would like one beer.   *Wǒ xiǎng yào yì bēi píjiǔ.*

3. We would like two glasses of water.

_____

4. We would like three theater tickets.

_____

Review the **shùzì** 1 through 20 and answer the following questions aloud, and then write the
numbers

answers in the blank spaces.

Zhěr yǒu dūoshǎo zhāng *(juhr) (yoh) (dwoh-show) (jahng)*   *sān*
are

zhūozi? *(jwoh-zuh)*
tables

Zhěr yǒu dūoshǎo *(juhr)*   _____
here

gè táidēng? *(guh)(ti-dung)*
(M)

Zhěr yǒu dūoshǎo bǎ yǐzi? *(bah)(yee-zuh)*   _____
(M)

ANSWERS

1. **Wǒ xiǎng yào qī zhāng míngxìnpiàn.**
2. **Wǒ xiǎng yào yì bēi píjiǔ.**
3. **Wǒmen xiǎng yào liǎng bēi shuǐ.**
4. **Wǒmen xiǎng yào sān zhāng xìpiào.**

(juhr) (yoh) (dwoh-show) (jung)
Zhèr yǒu dūoshǎo zhōng?
here   are   how many

_____

(jee)   (chwahng-hoo)
Zhèr yǒu jǐ gè chūanghù?
        how many (M)

_____

(jee)   (ruhn)
Zhèr yǒu jǐ gè rén?
        how many (M) people

liù

(nahn-ruhn)
Zhèr yǒu jǐ gè nánrén?
     (M)   men

_____

(new-ruhn)
Zhèr yǒu jǐ gè nǚrén?
     (M)   women

_____

(yahn-suh)
Yánsè
colors

Step 5

(yahn-suh)
Yánsè are the same in **Zhōngguó** as in **Měiguó** — they just have different **míngzì**.
colors   (may-gwoh) America   (meeng-zuh)

In **Zhōngguó,** there are many different customs regarding **yánsè**. For example,
                                                      (yahn-suh) colors

if you visit a **péngyou** in the hospital, you should take **hūar** that are **hóng** or **hūa**.
            (pung-yoh) friend   (hwar) flowers   (hohng) red   (hwah) multi-colored

Do not take **hūar** that are **bái** or **húang**—they are for mourning. Now let's learn the
                        (bi) white (hwahng) yellow

basic **yánsè**. Once you have read through the list on the next **ye,** cover the **Zhōngguó**
      colors   (yeh) page

zì with your hand and practice writing out the **Zhōngguó zì** next to the English **zì**.

13

(bi)
bái = white _____ **Chúan** (chwahn) **shì** (shr) **báide** (bi-duh).
boat   is

(hay)
hēi = black _____ **Qiu** (chee-yoo) **shì** **hēide** (hay-duh).
ball

(hwahng)
húang = yellow _____ **Xiangjiao** (ssee-ahng-jee-ow) **shì** **húangde** (hwahng-duh).
banana

(hohng)
hóng = red _____ *hóng* _____ **Shú** (shoo) **shì** **hóngde** (hohng-duh).
book

(lahn)
lán = blue _____ **Qìchē** (chee-chuh) **shì** **lánde** (lahn-duh).
car

(hwee)
hūi = gray _____ **Xìang** (ssee-ahng) **shì** **hūide** (hwee-duh).
elephant

(kah-fay)
kāfēi = brown _____ **Yǐzi** (yee-zuh) **shì** **kāfēide** (kah-fay-duh).
chair

(lew)
lǜ = green _____ **Cǎo** (tsow) **shì** **lǜde** (lew-duh).
grass

(fuhn)
fěn = pink _____ **Hùar** (hwar) **shì** **fěnde** (fuhn-duh).
flower

(hwah)
hūa = multi-colored _____ **Táidēng** (ti-dung) **shì** **hūade** (hwah-duh).
lamp

Now peel off the next set of labels and proceed to label the **yànsè** (yahn-suh) in your **fángzi** (fahng-zuh). Now
colors   house

let's practice using **zhè** (juh) **xīe** (ssee-eh) **zì**.
these   several

Bái (chwahn) **chúan** **zài** (zi) **nǎr** (nahr)? _____ *Bái* _____ **chúan** **zài** (zi) **nèr** (nuhr).
boat   is   where   is   there

Hēi (jwoh-zuh) **zhūozi** **zài** **nǎr**? _____ **zhūozi** **zài** **nèr**.
table

Kāfēi (yee-zuh) **yǐzi** **zài** **nǎr**? _____ **yǐzi** **zài** **nèr**.
chair

Bái (chee-yoo) **qíu** **zài** **nǎr**? _____ **qíu** **zài** **nèr**.
ball

Hūa (ti-dung) **táidēng** **zài** **nǎr**? _____ **táidēng** **zài** **nèr**.
lamp

Hóng (shoo) **shǔ** **zài** **nǎr**? _____ **shǔ** **zài** **nèr**.
book

(muhn) (zi) (nahr)
Lǚ mén zài nǎr?
door is where

_____ **mén zài něr.**
(zi) (nuhr)
is there

(fahng-zuh)
Fěn fángzi zài nǎr?
house

_____ **fángzi zài něr.**

(ssee-ahng-jee-ow)
Húang xiāngjiāo zài nǎr?
banana

_____ **xiāngjiāo zài něr.**

Note: In **Zhōngguó hùa**, "yǒu" means both "to have" and "there is/are."
(yoh)

(woh) (yoh)
wǒ yǒu = I have _____   **wǒmén yǒu** = we have _____
(woh-mun) (yoh)

Let's review **xiǎng yào** and learn **yǒu**. Be sure to repeat each sentence out loud.
(ssee-ahng) (yow)   (yoh)

(woh) (ssee-ahng) (yow) (bay) (pee-jee-oo)
Wǒ xiǎng yào yì bēi píjiǔ.
I would like one glass beer

(yoh)
Wǒ yǒu yì bēi píjiǔ.
I have beer

(woh-muhn)   **(jee-oo)**
Wǒmén xiǎng yào liǎng bēi jiǔ.
we would like wine

Wǒmén yǒu liǎng bēi jiǔ.
have wine

(shwee)
Wǒ xiǎng yào yì bēi shuǐ.
water

(swoh) (fahng-zuh)
Wǒ yǒu yì suǒ fángzi.
(M) house

(guh) (sah-lah)
Wǒmén xiǎng yào yí ge sālā.
(M) salad

(may-gwoh)
Wǒ zài Měiguó yǒu yì suǒ fángzi.
am in (M)

(chee-chuh)
Wǒmén xiǎng yào yí liàng qìchē.
(M)

(zuh-sseeng-chuh)
Wǒ yǒu yí liàng zìxíngchē.
(M) bicycle

(oh-joh)
Wǒmén xiǎng yào zài Ōuzhōu yǒu yí liàng qìchē.
to be in Europe have
(M) car

(oh-joh)
Wǒmén zài Ōuzhōu yǒu yí liàng qìchē.
Europe
(M) car

Now fill in the following blanks with the correct **zì** of **yǒu** or **xiǎng yào**.
form

Wǒmén yǒu _____
(we have)

sān liàng qìchē.
three (M)
(chee-chuh)

_____
(we would like)

liǎng zhǎng xìpiào.
two (M)
(jahng) (ssee-pee-ow)

_____
(I have)

yì zhǎng hùar.
one (M)
(hwar)

_____
(I would like)

qī zhǎng míngxìnpiàn.
seven (M)
(meeng-sseen-pee-ahn)

15

Zhèr shì yí gè quick review of the **yánsè.** Draw lines between **Zhōngguó zì** and the

(juhr) (shr) (M) *colors*

correct **yánsè.** On your mark, get set, *GO!*

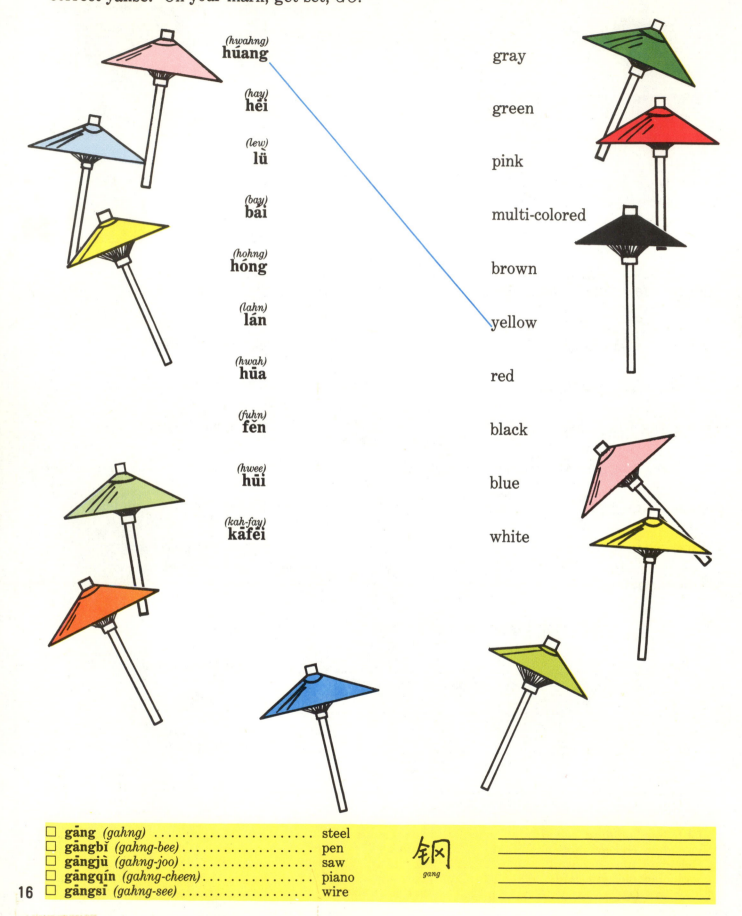

(hwahng)
húang

(hay)
hēi

(lew)
lǜ

(bay)
bái

(hohng)
hóng

(lahn)
lán

(hwah)
huā

(fuhn)
fěn

(hwee)
huī

(kah-fay)
kāfēi

gray

green

pink

multi-colored

brown

yellow

red

black

blue

white

☐ **gāng** *(gahng)* . . . . steel
☐ **gāngbǐ** *(gahng-bee)* . . . . pen
☐ **gāngjù** *(gahng-joo)* . . . . saw
☐ **gāngqín** *(gahng-cheen)* . . . . piano
16 ☐ **gāngsī** *(gahng-see)* . . . . wire

钢
gang

Pick up a language

in "10 Minutes a Day"®

TAKE A LANGUAGE BREAK

for "10 Minutes a Day"®

LEARN A LANGUAGE *in* "10 MINUTES A DAY"®

(chee-ahn)
Qían
money

Before starting this Step, go back and review Step 4. Make sure you can count to èrshí *(ur-shr)* *twenty*

without looking back at the shū *(shoo)* *book*. Let's learn the larger shùzì *(shoo-zuh)* *numbers* now, so if something

costs more than 20 yúan *(yoo-ahn)*, you will know exactly how much it costs. After practicing aloud

Zhōngwén *(jung-wuhn)* *Chinese* shùzì *(shoo-zuh)* *numbers* 10 through 100 below, write these shùzì *(shoo-zuh)* in the blanks provided.

Again, notice the similarities between numbers such as wǔshí *(woo-shr)* (50), wǔ *(woo)* (5) and shíwǔ *(shr-woo)* (15).

10	shi *(shr)*	(sí *(see)*	+ lìu *(lee-oo)*	=	shí) *(shr)*
20	èrshí *(ur-shr)*	(èr *(ur)*		=	2)
30	sānshí *(sahn-shr)*	(sān *(sahn)*		=	3)
40	sìshí *(see-shr)*	(sì *(see)*		=	4)
50	wǔshí *(woo-shr)*	(wǔ *(woo)*		=	5)
60	liùshi *(lee-oo-shr)*	(lìu *(lee-oo)*		=	6)
70	qīshí *(chee-shr)*	(qī *(chee)*		=	7)
80	bāshí *(bah-shr)*	(bā *(bah)*		=	8)
90	jiǔshí *(jee-oo-shr)*	(jiǔ *(jee-oo)*		=	9)
100	yībǎi *(yee-bi)*				
1000	yīqiān *(yee-chee-ahn)*				

10 _____ *shí*
20 _____
30 _____
40 _____
50 _____
60 _____
70 _____
80 _____
90 _____
100 _____
1000 _____

Now take a logical guess. Zěnme *(zuhn-muh)* *how* would you write (and say) the following? The answers

zài *(zi)* *are at* the bottom of zhèi yè *(juh-ay)(yeh)* *this page*.

400 _____   600 _____

2000 _____   5300 _____

The unit of currency in **Zhōngguó** *(jung-gwoh)* is the **yúan** *(yoo-ahn)*. Currency is called **zhǐbì** *(juhr-bee)* and coins are
China

called **yìngbì** *(yeeng-bee)*. Just as in **Měiguó** *(may-gwoh)* where a dollar can be broken down into 100 pennies,
America

the **yúan** *(yoo-ahn)* can be divided into 100 **fēn** *(fuhn)*. The **yúan** *(yoo-ahn)* can also be broken down into 10 **jiao** *(jee-ow)*

or **máo** *(mow)*. **Jiao** *(jee-ow)*, or **máo** *(mow)*, and **fēn** *(fuhn)* are also called **fūbì** *(foo-bee)*. Let's learn the various kinds of

zhǐbì *(juhr-bee)* and **yìngbì** *(yeeng-bee)*. Because you will not be able to exchange American currency for **yúan**
currency   coins

until you are actually in China, study the pictures below to familiarize yourself with the

various **zhǐbì** *(juhr-bee)* and **yìngbì** *(yeeng-bee)*. Also make sure to practice each **zì** *(zuh)* out loud.
currency   coins   word

Zhǐbì *(juhr-bee)*

yī jiao *(yee) (jee-ow)*
one   jiao

èr jiao/mao *(ur) (jee-ow)*
two   jiao

wǔ jiao/mao *(woo) (jee-ow)*
five   jiao

yī yúan/kuai *(yee) (yoo-ahn)*
one   yuan

liǎng yúan *(lee-ahng) (yoo-ahn)*
two   yuan

wǔ yúan *(woo) (yoo-ahn)*
five   yuan

shí yúan *(shr) (yoo-ahn)*
ten   yuan

Yìngbì *(yeeng-bee)*

yī fēn *(yee) (fuhn)*
one   fen

èr fēn *(ur) (fuhn)*
two   fen

wǔ fēn *(woo) (fuhn)*
five   fen

☐ **nián** *(nee-ahn)*	year	
☐ **jīn nián** *(jeen) (nee-ahn)*	this year	年
☐ **míng nián** *(meeng) (nee-ahn)*	next year	*nian*
☐ **qù nián** *(chee-oo) (nee-ahn)*	last year	
☐ **sān nián** *(sahn) (nee-ahn)* . . . . . three years		

Review the **shùzì** *(shoo-zuh)* **shí** *(shr)* through **yīqiān** *(yee-chee-ahn)* again. Now, in **Zhōngwén,** *(jung-wuhn)* **nǐ** *(nee)* **zěnme shuō** *(zuhn-muh)(shwoh)*

numbers *ten* *one thousand* *Chinese* *you* *how say*

"twenty-two" or "fifty-three"? You actually do a bit of arithmetic — 5 times 10 plus 3 *wǔ shí sān*

equals 53. See if you can say and write out the **shùzì** *(shoo-zuh)* on **zhèi** *(juh-ay)* **yè.** *(yeh)* The answers **zài** *(zi)*
wǔshísān *this* *are at*

the bottom of the **yè.** *(yeh)*
page

a.	25 = *èrshíwǔ*	(2 x 10) + 5
b.	47 =	(4 x 10) + 7
c.	84 =	(8 x 10) + 4
d.	51 =	(5 x 10) + 1

e.	36 =	(3 x 10) + 6
f.	93 =	(9 x 10) + 3
g.	68 =	(6 x 10) + 8
h.	72 =	(7 x 10) + 2

To ask how much something costs in **Zhōngguó hùa,** *(jung-gwoh)* *(hwah)* one asks, **"Dūoshǎo qían?"** *(dwoh-show)* *(chee-ahn)* **Xìanzài** *(ssee-ahn-zi)*

Chinese *language* *how much* *money* *now*

answer the following questions based on the **shùzì** *(shoo-zuh)* in parentheses.
numbers

1. **Nà ge dūoshǎo qían?** *(nah) (guh)(dwoh-show) (chee-ahn)*   **Nà** *(nah)* *shí* **yúan.** *(yoo-ahn)*
   that *(M)* *how much* *money*   (10)

2. **Nà ge dūoshǎo qían?** *(nah) (guh)(dwoh-show) (chee-ahn)*   **Nà** *(nah)* _____ **yúan.** *(yoo-ahn)*
   that *(M)* *how much* *money*   (20)

3. **Nà běn shū dūoshǎo qían?** *(buhn) (shoo) (dwoh-show) (chee-ahn)*   **Nà** _____ **yúan.**
   that *(M)* *book*   (17)

4. **Nà lǐang qìchē dūoshǎo qían?** *(lee-ahng)(chee-chuh) (dwoh-show)*   **Nà** _____ **yúan.**
   (M) *car*   (2000)

5. **Nà zhāng zhàopìan dūoshǎo qían?** *(jahng) (jow-pee-ahn)*   **Nà** _____ **yúan.**
   (M) *photo*   (5)

6. **Nà jīan wūzi dūoshǎo qían?** *(jee-ahn) (woo-zuh)*   **Nà** _____ **yúan.**
   (M) *room*   (24)

7. **Nà zhāng hùar dūoshǎo qían?** *(jahng) (hwar)*   **Nà** _____ **yúan.**
   (M) *picture*   (923)

Step 7

(jeen-tee-ahn) *(meeng-tee-ahn)* *(zwoh-tee-ahn)*
Jīntiān, Míngtiān, Zúotiān
today   tomorrow   yesterday

(rur-lee) **Rìlì** calendar						
(yee) **Yī** one	*(guh)* **ge** (M)	*(sseeng-chee)* **xīngqī** week	*(yoh)* **yŏu** has	*(chee)* **qī** seven	*(tee-ahn)* **tiān.** days	
(sseeng-chee-yee) **xīngqīyī** 1	*(sseeng-chee-ur)* **xīngqīer** 2	*(sseeng-chee-sahn)* **xīngqīsan** 3	*(sseeng-chee-see)* **xīngqīsì** 4	*(sseeng-chee-woo)* **xīngqīwŭ** 5	*(sseeng-chee-lee-oo)* **xīngqīliù** 6	*(sseeng-chee-tee-ahn)* **xīngqītiān** 7

Notice that, in *(jung-wuhn)* **Zhōngwén**, numbers are included in the names for weekdays. It is *(huhn)* **hĕn** very important to know these days. Be sure to say them aloud before filling in the blanks below.

(sseeng-chee-yee)
xīngqīyī *xīngqīyī*   *(sseeng-chee-ur)* **xīngqīer** _____
Monday   Tuesday

(sseeng-chee-sahn)
xīngqīsan _____   *(sseeng-chee-see)* **xīngqīsì** _____
Wednesday   Thursday

(sseeng-chee-woo)
xīngqīwŭ _____   *(sseeng-chee-lee-oo)* **xīngqīliù** _____
Friday   Saturday

(sseeng-chee-tee-ahn)
xīngqītiān _____
Sunday

(jeen-tee-ahn) *(shr)* *(sseeng-chee-see)* *(meeng-tee-ahn)* *(sseeng-chee-woo)* *(zwoh-tee-ahn)* *(sseeng-chee-sahn)*
If **jīntiān** **shì** **xīngqīsì**, then **míngtiān shì xīngqīwŭ** and **zúotiān shì xīngqīsan**. Now,
today is Thursday   tomorrow is Friday   yesterday was Wednesday

(sseeng-chee-see)
you supply the correct answers. If **jīntiān shì xīngqīsì**, then **míngtiān shì** _____
today Thursday   tomorrow

and **zúotiān shì** _____. Or, if **jīntiān shì xīngqīsì**, then *míngtiān*
yesterday   today Thursday

(sseeng-chee-woo) *(sseeng-chee-sahn)*
shì xīngqīwŭ and _____ **shì xīngqīsan**. Easy, wasn't it? **Jīntiān shì**
Friday   Wednesday   today

_____.

(ssee-ahn-zi) *(chee)* *(guh)* *(rur-lee)*
Xìanzài, peel off the next **qī** **ge** labels and put them on the **rìlì** that you use every day.
now   seven (M)   calendar

(shr) *(sseeng-chee-yee)*
From now on, Monday **shì xīngqīyī!**
is

☐ **là** *(lah)*	wax		_____
☐ **làbĭ** *(lah-bee)*	crayon		_____
☐ **làtái** *(lah-ti)*	candlestick	蜡	_____
☐ **làzhĭ** *(lah-juhr)*	waxpaper	la	_____
☐ **làzhú** *(lah-joo)*	candle		_____

There are **sì** **gè** parts to each **tiān**.
(see)(guh) four (M)   *(tee-ahn)* day

morning = **shàngwǔ** _____
(shahng-woo)

afternoon = **xìawǔ** *xiawu* _____
(ssee-ah-woo)

evening = **wǎnshang** _____
(wahn-shahng)

night = **yèlǐ** _____
(yeh-lee)

Also, in **Zhōngwén**, **báitiān** means daytime. **Xìanzài**, fill in the following blanks
(jung-wuhn)   *(bi-tee-ahn)*   *(ssee-ahn-zi)* now

and then check your answers at the bottom of **zhèi yè**.
(juh-ay)(yeh) this   page

a. Sunday morning = _____

b. Friday evening = _____

c. Saturday evening = _____

d. Monday morning = _____

e. Wednesday morning = _____

f. Tuesday afternoon = _____

g. Thursday afternoon = _____

h. Thursday night = _____*xīngqīsì yèlǐ*_____

i. yesterday evening = _____

j. this afternoon = _____
(today)

k. this morning = _____

l. tomorrow afternoon = _____

m. tomorrow evening = _____

ANSWERS

a. xīngqītiān shàngwǔ	e. xīngqīsān shàngwǔ	i. zuótiān wǎnshang
b. xīngqīwǔ wǎnshang	f. xīngqíèr xìawǔ	j. jīntiān xìawǔ
c. xīngqīliù wǎnshang	g. xīngqīsì xìawǔ	k. jīntiān shàngwǔ
d. xīngqīyī shàngwǔ	h. xīngqīsì yèlǐ	l. míngtiān xìawǔ
		m. míngtiān wǎnshang

21

So, with merely **shíyī** *(shr-yee)* **ge** *(guh)* **zì** *(zuh)*, you can specify any day of the **xīngqī** *(sseeng-chee)* and any time of the

week

tiān. *(tee-ahn)* The words **"jīntiān,"** *(jeen-tee-ahn)* **"míngtiān"** *(meeng-tee-ahn)* and **"zuótiān"** *(zwoh-tee-ahn)* will be **hěn** *(huhn)* important in making

day · today · tomorrow · yesterday · very

reservations and appointments, in getting **xìpiào** *(ssee-pee-ow)* and for many other things you will want

theater tickets

to do. Knowing the parts of the **tiān** will help you to understand the various forms of

day

"good-bye" in **Zhōngguó hùa.** *(hwah)*

language

see you tomorrow =	**míngtiān jìan** *(meeng-tee-ahn)(jee-ahn)*
see you in the afternoon =	**xìawǔ jìan** *(ssee-ah-woo)(jee-ahn)*
see you in the evening =	**wǎnshàng jìan** *(wahn-shahng)(jee-ahn)*
see you tomorrow afternoon =	**míngtiān xìawǔ jìan** *(meeng-tee-ahn)(ssee-ah-woo)(jee-ahn)*

xìawǔ jìan

Take the next **sì** *(see)* **ge** labels and stick them on the appropriate things in your **fángzi.** *(fahng-zuh)*

four (M) · house

What about the bathroom mirror for **"míngtiān jìan"**? Or a wall clock for **"xìawǔ jìan"**?

Remember that, in **Zhōngguó,** *(jung-gwoh)* people do not say "good morning," "good afternoon" or

"good night." You may be greeted with **"Nǐ hǎo?"** *(nee)(how)*, meaning "How are you?"

you · good

In **Zhōngguó,** you are much more likely to hear a form of "good-bye" like **"zài jìan,"** *(zì)(jee-ahn)*

which means "See you again." If you really want to enjoy **Zhōngguó,** *(jung-gwoh)* learn the different

forms of "good-bye"—you will hear them often.

You are about one-fourth of your way through **zhèi běn shu** *(juh-ay)(buhn)(shoo)* and it is a good time to

this (M) · book

quickly review the **zì** *(zuh)* you have learned before doing the crossword puzzle on the next page.

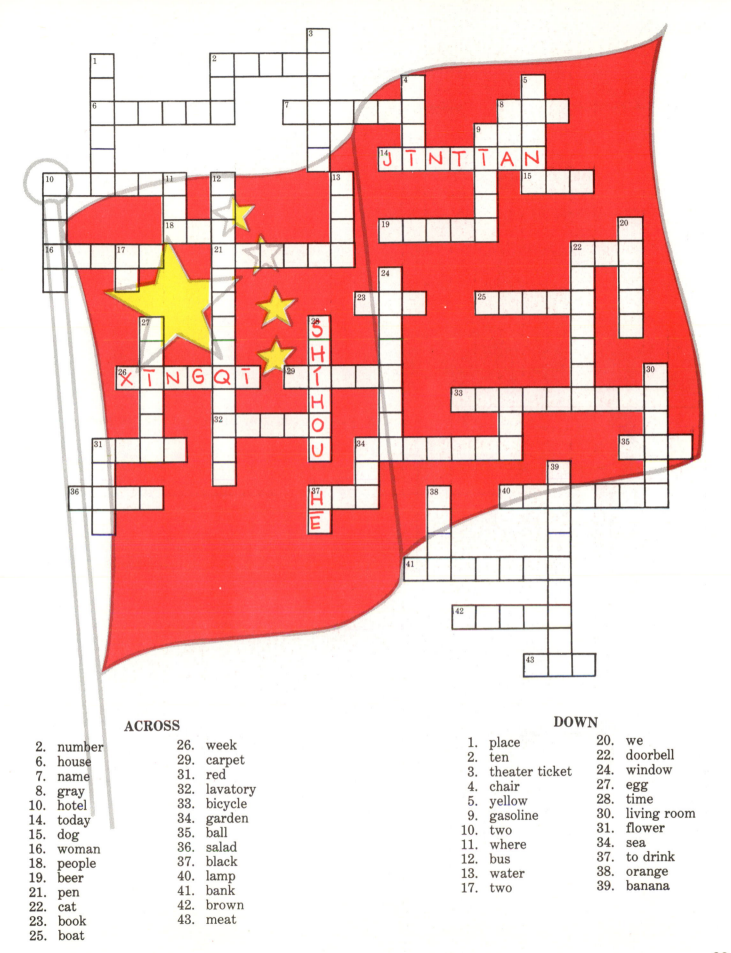

ACROSS

2. number
6. house
7. name
8. gray
10. hotel
14. today
15. dog
16. woman
18. people
19. beer
21. pen
22. cat
23. book
25. boat
26. week
29. carpet
31. red
32. lavatory
33. bicycle
34. garden
35. ball
36. salad
37. black
40. lamp
41. bank
42. brown
43. meat

DOWN

1. place
2. ten
3. theater ticket
4. chair
5. yellow
9. gasoline
10. two
11. where
12. bus
13. water
17. two
20. we
22. doorbell
24. window
27. egg
28. time
30. living room
31. flower
34. sea
37. to drink
38. orange
39. banana

23

Step 8

Lǐ, Shàng, Wài
(lee) *(shahng)* *(wi)*
inside   on   outside

While in **Zhōngguó** *(jung-gwoh)*, the use of prepositions (words like "in," "on," "through," and "next to") will allow you to be precise with a minimum amount of effort. Instead of having to point **liù** *(lee-oo)* / six times at a piece of jewelry you wish to buy, you can explain precisely which piece you want by saying **zài** / it is   behind, in front of, next to, or under the jewelry that the salesperson is starting to pick up. Let's learn some of these little **zì** *(zuh)* that are **hěn** *(huhn)* / very similar to **Yīngwén** *(yeeng-wuhn)* / English. Study the examples below.

cong *(tswong)* = from	**pangbianr** *(pahng-bee-ahnr)* = next to	**xiabianr** *(ssee-ah-bee-ahnr)* = under
	by side	under side
jìn *(jeen)* = into, in	**lǐ** = inside	**shangbianr** *(shahng-bee-ahnr)* = over
		top side

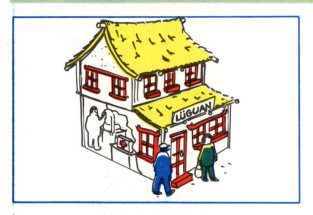

(nah) *(guh)* *(nahn-ruhn)*(*zoh*) *(jeen)*   *(sseen)* *(lew-gwahn)*
Nà ge nánrén zou jìn nà ge xīn lǚguǎn.
that   (M)   man   enters into   new   hotel

(nah) *(guh)* *(new-ruhn)* *(tswong)*   *(how)* *(lew-gwahn)*(*choo*) *(li)*
Nà ge nǚrén cóng nà ge hǎo lǚguǎn chū lái.
that   (M)   woman   from   good   hotel   out   come

      (yee-shuhng) *(zi)*   *(how)*   *(lee)*
Nà ge yīshēng zài nà ge hǎo lǚguǎn lǐ.
      doctor   is   good   hotel   inside

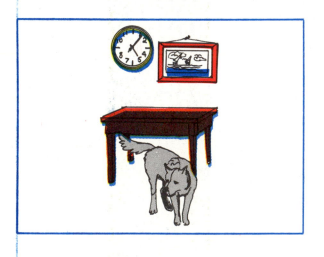

(nah) *(jahng)* *(sseen)* *(hwar)* *(zi)* *(jwoh-zuh)* *(shahng-bee-ahnr)*
Nà zhāng xīn hùar zài zhuōzi shàngbianr.
that   (M)   new   picture   is   table   over
(nah) *(jahng)*   *(zi)* *(jung)* *(pahng-bee-ahnr)*
Nà zhāng xīn hùar zài zhōng pángbianr.
    (M)   new   picture   is   clock   next to
            (kah-fay) *(jwoh-zuh)*   *(hwar)* *(ssee-ah-bee-ahnr)*
Nà ge kāfēi zhuōzi zài hùar xiabianr.
       brown   table   is   picture   under
        (hwee)(*goh*)   *(jwoh-zuh)* *(pahng-bee-ahnr)*
Nà ge hūi gǒu zài zhuōzi pángbianr.
       gray   dog   table   next to
       (lew) *(jung)*   *(jwoh-zuh)* *(shahng-bee-ahnr)*
Nà ge lǚ zhōng zài zhuōzi shàngbianr.
     green clock   table   over
       (lew) *(jung)*   *(hwar)* *(pahng-bee-ahnr)*
Nà ge lǚ zhōng zài hùar pángbianr.
     green clock   picture   next to

☐ **cài** *(tsi)* . . . . vegetable
☐ **báicài** *(bi-tsi)* . . . . cabbage
☐ **bōcài** *(bwo-tsi)* . . . . spinach
☐ **qíncài** *(cheen-tsi)* . . . . celery
☐ **shēngcài** *(shung-tsi)* . . . . lettuce

菜
cai

24

_____
_____
_____
_____
_____

Fill in the blanks below with the correct preposition according to the **hùar** *(hwar)* on the *picture* previous **yè.** *(yeh) page*

Nà ge nánrén zǒu _____ **nà ge xīn lüguǎn.**
that *(nahn-ruhn)* *man* *(zoh)* *enters* *(sseen)* *new* *(lew-gwahn)* *hotel*

Nà ge hūi gǒu zài zhuōzi _____.
(M) *(hwee)* *gray* *(goh)* *dog* *(zi)* *is* *(jwoh-zuh)* *table*

Nà ge lü zhōng zài zhuōzi *shàngbiānr.*
that *(lew)* *green* *(jung)* *clock* *table* *(jwoh-zuh)*

Nà zhāng xīn hùar zài zhuōzi _____.
new *(sseen)* *picture* *(hwar)* *is* *table* *(jwoh-zuh)*

Nà ge lü zhōng zài hùar _____.
that *(lew)* *green* *(jung)* *clock* *picture* *(hwar)*

Nà ge yīshēng zài nà ge hǎo lüguǎn
(M) *(yee-shuhng)* *doctor* *is* *(how)* *good* *(lew-gwahn)* *hotel*

Nà zhāng kāfēi zhuōzi zài hùar _____.
(M) *(jahng)* *brown* *(kah-fay)* *table* *(jwoh-zuh)* *is* *picture* *(hwar)*

_____.

Nà zhāng xīn huar zài zhōng _____.
new *picture* *is*

Xiànzài, answer these questions based on the **hùar** on the previous **yè.** Notice that the
(ssee-ahn-zi) *now* *picture* *page*

word **"ma"** is often used at the end of questions.
(mah)

Yīshēng zài nǎr? _____
(yee-shuhng) *(zi)* *(nahr)*
doctor *is* *where*

Gǒu zài nǎr? *Nà ge gǒu zài zhuōzi pángbiānr.*
(goh) *(zi)* *(nahr)*
dog *is* *where*

Zhuōzi zài nǎr? _____
(jwoh-zuh) *(nahr)*
table *is* *where*

Hùar zài nǎr? _____
(hwar) *(nahr)*
picture *is* *where*

Nà ge nürén zài zuò shénme? _____
(new-ruhn) *(zoh)* *(shun-muh)*
that *woman* *is* *doing* *what*

Nà ge nánrén zài zuò shénme? _____
(nahn-ruhn) *(zoh)*
that *man* *is* *doing* *what*

Zhōng shì lüde ma? _____
(jung) *(shr)* *(lew-duh)* *(mah)*
clock *is* *green*

Gǒu shì hūide ma? _____
(goh) *(hwee-duh)* *(mah)*
dog *is* *gray*

Xiànzài *(ssee-ahn-zi)* for some more practice with **Zhōngwén** *(jung-wuhn)* prepositions.
now

> **shàng** *(shahng)* = on top of (horizontal surface), on (vertical surface)
>
> **qiánbianr** *(chee-ahn-bee-ahnr)* = in front of
> front   side
>
> **hòubianr** *(hoh-bee-ahnr)* = behind
> rear   side

Nà bēi shǔi zài zhūozi shàng.
that glass water is table on
(shwee) (jwoh-zuh) (shahng)

Nà zhāng kāfēi hùar zài qíang shàng.
that (M) brown picture is wall on
(kah-fay) (chee-ahng)

Nà ge húang dēng zài zhūozi hòubianr.
that (M) yellow lamp table behind
(hwahng) (dung) (jwoh-zuh) (hoh-bee-ahnr)

Nà ge kāfēi zhūozi zài chúang qiánbianr.
that (M) brown table bed in front of
(chwahng) (chee-ahn-bee-ahnr)

Nà ge hūa chúang zài kāfēi zhūozi hòubianr.
that (M) multi-colored bed brown table behind
(hwah) (chwahng) (hoh-bee-ahnr)

Nà bēi shǔi zài zhūozi _shàng_ .
(jwoh-zuh)

Nà zhāng kāfēi hùar zài qíang _____ .
(chee-ahng)

Nà ge húang dēng zài zhūozi _____ .

Nà ge kāfēi zhūozi zài chúang _____ .

Nà ge hūa chúang zài kāfēi zhūozi _____

_____ .

Answer the following **wèntí** *(wuhn-tee)*, based on the **hùar** *(hwar)*, by filling in the blanks with the correct
questions picture

prepositions from those you have just learned.

Nà běn hóng shū zài nǎr? *(nah) (buhn) (hohng) (shoo) (zi) (nahr)*
that (M) red book is where

Lán gōnggòngqìchē zài nǎr? *(lahn) (goong-goong-chee-chuh)*
blue bus is where

Nà běn hóng shū zài kāfēi zhūozi _____ .
brown   table   *(jwoh-zuh)*

Lán gōnggòngqìchē zài hūi lügǔan _____ .
gray   hotel   *(hwee) (lew-gwahn)*

☐ **shí** *(shr)* . . . . to eat
☐ **shíwù** *(shr-woo)* . . . . food
☐ **shípǔ** *(shr-poo)* . . . . cookbook, recipes
☐ **shíyù** *(shr-yoo)* . . . . appetite
☐ **shílíang** *(shr-lee-ahng)* . . . . foodstuff, grain

食
shi

(hwee) *(dee-ahn-hwah)* *(lew)* *(dee-tahn)* *(hwar)*
Huī dianhua zai nar? Lǜ ditan zai nar? Huar zai nar?
gray   telephone   is   where   green   carpet   picture

(hwee)(dee-ahn-hwah) *(bi)* *(chee-ahng)*
Nà ge huī dianhua zai bái qiang _____ .
     gray   telephone   white   wall

(hwah)
Nà ge huī dianhua zai huā   huar _____ .
     gray   telephone   multi-colored picture

(hay) *(jwoh-zuh)*
Nà ge huī dianhua zai hēi zhūozi _____ .
     gray   telephone   black   table

(lew) *(dee-tahn)* *(hay)*
Nà ge lǜ ditan zai hēi zhūozi _____ .
     green   carpet   black   table

(bi) *(chee-ahng)*
Nà zhāng huar zai bái qiang   _shàng_ _____ .
   (M)   picture   white   wall

(ssee-ahn-zi) *(lew-gwahn)*
Xianzai fill in each blank on the **lǚguǎn** below with the best preposition. The correct
now   hotel

(zi) *(juh-ay)(yeh)*
answers **zai** the bottom of **zhei ye.** Have fun.
   are at   this   page

旅馆

lǚguǎn

1. _____

2. _____

6. _lǐ_ _____

3. _____

10. _____

4. _____

7. _____

8. _____

9. _____

5. _____

ANSWERS

1. **shàngbianr**	3. **houbianr**	5. **jìn**	7. **pángbianr**	9. **xiàbianr**
2. **shàng**	4. **shàng**	6. **lǐ**	8. **dianbianr**	10. **cóng**

27

Step 9

(see-yoo-eh) (lee-oo-yoo-eh) (jee-oo-yoo-eh) (shr-yee-yoo-eh) (doh) (yoh) (sahn-shr) (tee-ahn)

Sìyùe, liùyùe, jiǔyùe, shíyīyue dōu yǒu sānshi tiān.
April   June   September   November   all   have   thirty   days

Sound familiar? You have learned the days of **(sseeng-chee)** **xīngqī,** so **(ssee-ahn-zi)** **xiànzài** is the time to learn the
week — now

(yoo-eh) **(nee-ahn)**
yùe of the **nían** and all the different kinds of **(tee-ahn-chee)** **tiānqì** that you may encounter on your
months — year — weather

holiday. For example, you ask about the **(tee-ahn-chee)** **tiānqì** in **(jung-wuhn)** **Zhōngwén** a little differently than you
weather

do in **(yeeng-wuhn)** **Yīngwén** — **(jeen-tee-ahn) (tee-ahn-chee) (yahng)** "**Jīntiān tiānqì zěnme yàng?**" Practice all the possible answers
English — today — weather — how — kind

to this **(wuhn-tee)** **wèntí** and then write the following answers in the blanks below.
question

(tee-ahn-chee)
Jīntiān tiānqì zěmme yàng?

(jeen-tee-ahn) (ssee-ah-yoo)
Jīntiān xìayǔ _____
today — rains

(ssee-ah-ssee-yoo-eh)
Jīntiān xìaxǔe _____
today — snows

(noo-ahn-huh)
Jīntiān nǔanhe _____
warm

(lung)
Jīntiān lěng _____
cold

(tee-ahn-chee) (how)
Jīntiān tiānqì hǎo *Jīntiān tiānqì hǎo.* _____
weather — good

(tee-ahn-chee) (boo-how)
Jīntiān tiānqì bùhǎo _____
weather — not good

(ruh)
Jīntiān re _____
hot

(ssee-ah-woo)
Jīntiān xìawù _____
foggy

Xìanzài practice the **Zhōngwén** **(zuh)** **zì** on the next **yè** aloud and then fill in the blanks with
words — page

the **(meeng-zuh)** **míngzi** of the **(yoo-eh)** **yùe** and the appropriate **(tee-ahn-chee)** **tiānqì** report. Notice that a number precedes
names — months — weather

the word for month, **(yoo-eh)** **yùe,** in **Zhōngguó.** For example, **(sahn-yoo-eh)** **sānyùe** means third or March.

☐ **gúo** (gwoh)	nation, state	
☐ **Fǎguó** (fah-gwoh)	France	
☐ **Měiguó** (may-gwoh)	America	王 guo
☐ **Yīngguó** (yeeng-gwoh)	England	
☐ **Zhōngguó** (jung-gwoh)	China	

(yee-yoo-eh) **yīyuè** _____ January	*(ssee-ah-ssee-yoo-eh)* **Yīyuè xiàxuě.** _____ snows
(ur-yoo-eh) **èryuè** _____ February	*(yuh)* *(ssee-ah-ssee-yoo-eh)* **Èryuè yě xiàxuě.** _____ also snows
(sahn-yoo-eh) **sānyuè** _____ March	*(ssee-ah-yoo)* **Sānyuè xiàyǔ.** *Sānyùe xiàyǔ.* rains
(see-yoo-eh) **sìyuè** _____ April	*(yuh)* *(ssee-ah-yoo)* **Sìyuè yě xiàyǔ.** _____ also rains
(woo-yoo-eh) **wǔyuè** _____ May	*(gwah-fung)* **Wǔyuè guāfēng.** _____ windy
(lee-oo-yoo-eh) **liùyuè** *liùyùe* June	*(yuh)* *(gwah-fung)* **Liùyuè yě guāfēng.** _____ also windy
(chee-yoo-eh) **qīyuè** _____ July	*(huhn)(noo-ahn-huh)* **Qīyuè hěn nuǎnhe.** _____ very warm
(bah-yoo-eh) **bāyuè** _____ August	*(ruh)* **Bāyuè hěn rè.** _____ very hot
(jee-oo-yoo-eh) **jiǔyuè** _____ September	*(tee-ahn-chee) (how)* **Jiǔyuè tiānqì hǎo.** _____ weather good
(shr-yoo-eh) **shíyuè** _____ October	*(chahng-chahng) (ssee-ah-woo)* **Shíyuè chángcháng xiàwù.** _____ often foggy
(shr-yee-yoo-eh) **shíyīyuè** _____ November	*(huhn)(lung)* **Shíyīyuè hěn lěng.** _____ very cold
(shr-ur-yoo-eh) **shíèryuè** _____ December	*(tee-ahn-chee) (boo-how)* **Shíèryuè tiānqì hěn bùhǎo.** _____ _____ weather very not good

(ssee-ahn-zi)
Xiànzài answer the following *(wuhn-tee)* **wèntí** based on the **huàr** to the right.
now   questions   picture

(ur-yoo-eh) *(yahng)*
Èryuè tiānqì zěnme yàng? _____
February weather how kind

(see-yoo-eh) *(yahng)*
Sìyuè tiānqì zěnme yàng? _____
April how kind

(woo-yoo-eh) *(yahng)*
Wǔyuè tiānqì zěnme yàng? _____
May kind

(bah-yoo-eh)
Bāyuè tiānqì zěnme yàng? _____
August

(how) (boo-how)
Tiānqì hǎo bùhǎo? _____
weather good not good

Xìanzài for the seasons of the **nían . . .**
now   year

(dwong-tee-ahn)
dōngtiān
winter

dōngtiān

(ssee-tee-ahn)
xiàtiān
summer

(chee-yoo-tee-ahn)
qiūtiān
autumn

(chun-tee-ahn)
chūntiān
spring

(lung)
Dōngtiān lěng.
winter   cold

(ruh)
Xiàtiān rè.
summer   hot

(gwah-fung)
Qiūtiān gūafēng.
autumn   windy

(chahng-chahng)
Chūntiān chángcháng
spring   often
(ssee-ah-yoo)
xìayǔ.
rains

At this point, it is a good time to familiarize yourself with **Zhōngguó** *(chee-wuhn)* **qìwěn.** temperatures

Carefully read the typical *(tee-ahn-chee)* **tiānqi** forecasts below and study the thermometer because weather

temperatures in **Zhōngguó** are calculated on the basis of Centigrade (not Fahrenheit).

(hwah-shr)
húashì
Fahrenheit

(shuh-shr)
shèshì
Centigrade

212° F —— 100° C	*(shwee) (ki)* **shǔi kāi** water boils
98.6° F —— 37° C	*(jung-chahng)* **zhèngcháng** *(tee-wuhn)* **tiwěn** normal body temperature
68° F —— 20° C	
32° F —— 0° C	*(shwee) (beeng) (dee-ahn)* **shǔi bīng dǐan** water freezing point
0° F —— -17.8° C	*(yahn) (shwee) (beeng) (dee-ahn)* **yán shǔi bīng dǐan** salt water freezing point
-10° F —— -23.3° C	

(sahn-yoo-eh)(ur-shr) *(sseng-chee-yee)* *(shr)*
Sānyùe èrshí, xīngqīyī tiānqì shì:
March   20   Monday   weather   is

(lung) *(gwah-fung)*
lěng, gūafēng
cold   windy
(chee-wuhn) *(doo)*
qìwěn   5 dù
temperature   degrees

(chee-yoo-eh) *(shr-bah)* *(sseng-chee-sahn)*
Qíyùe   shíbā, xīngqīsān tiānqì shì:
July   18   Wednesday   weather

(noo-ahn) (cheeng)
nǔan, qíng
warm   fine
(chee-wuhn) *(doo)*
qìwěn   20 dù
temperature   degrees

guo

(jee-ah) *(tee-ahn)* *(mee)* *(duh)* *(jee-ah)*
Jīa — Tían mì de Jīa
home   sweet   home

Step 10

In **Zhōngguó,** not just the parents, but also the grandparents, aunts, uncles and cousins are all considered as close family, so let's take a look at the **zì** for them. Study the family tree below and then write out the **xīn zì** *(sseen)* in the blanks that follow. Notice that, new in **Zhōngguó,** the family name comes first, and the given name (or what we, in **Měiguó,** *(may-gwoh)* America think of as the first name) follows.

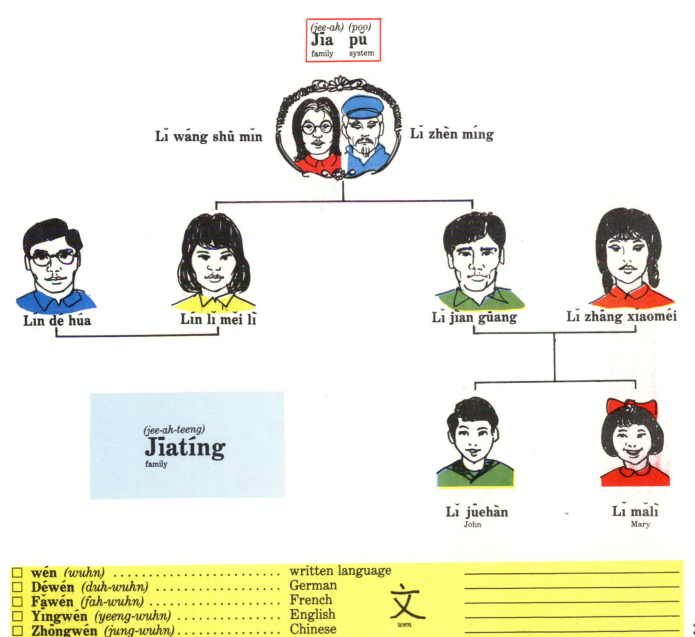

(jee-ah) *(poo)*
Jīa   pu
family   system

Lǐ wáng shū mǐn   Lǐ zhèn míng

Lǐn dé húa   Lín lì mei lì   Lǐ jīan gǔang   Lǐ zhāng xīaoméi

(jee-ah-teeng)
Jīatíng
family

Lǐ júehàn
John

Lǐ mǎlì
Mary

☐ **wén** *(wuhn)*	written language	文 *wen*	_____
☐ **Déwén** *(duh-wuhn)*	German		_____
☐ **Fǎwén** *(fah-wuhn)*	French		_____
☐ **Yīngwén** *(yeeng-wuhn)*	English		_____
☐ **Zhōngwén** *(jung-wuhn)*	Chinese		_____

31

(zoo-foo-moo)
zǔfùmǔ
grandparents

(foo-moo)
fùmǔ
parents

(zoo-foo)
zǔfù
grandfather
zǔfù

(foo-cheen)
fùqin
father

(zoo-moo)
zǔmǔ
grandmother

(moo-cheen)
mǔqin
mother

(ssee-ow-hahr)
xiǎohár
children

(ur-zuh)
érzi
son

(cheen-chee)
qīnqì
relatives

(shoo-shoo)
shūshu
uncle

(new-ur)
nǚér
daughter

(goo-goo)
gūgu
aunt

(ur-zuh) *(new-ur)* *(guh-guh)* *(may-may)*
Érzi and **nǚér** are also **gēge** and **mèimei.**
son　　　daughter　　　brother　　　sister

Let's learn **zěnme** to identify family members by **míngzi.** Study the following examples.
how
(meeng-zuh)
name

(foo-cheen)(jee-ow)
Fùqin jiào shénme ?
father　called　what

Fùqin jiào _Lín dé húa_ .

(moo-cheen)(jee-ow)
Mǔqin jiào shénme ?
mother　called　what

Mǔqin jiào _____ .

Xìanzài you fill in the blanks, based on the **hùar,** in the same manner.
now
picture

Érzi

(jee-ow)
jiào shénme ?
called　what

_____ jiào _____ .

(jee-ow)
jiào shénme ?
called　what

_____ jiào _Mǎlì_ .

32

Study all these *(hwar)* **hùar** and then practice pictures

saying and writing out the *(zuh)* **zì.** words

(juh) (shr) (choo-fahng)
Zhè shì chúfáng.
this is   kitchen

(beeng-ssee-ahng)
bīngxiāng
refrigerator

(loo-zuh)
lúzi
stove

lúzi

(jee-oo)
jiǔ
wine

(pee-jee-oo)
píjiǔ
beer

(nee-oo-ni)
niúnǎi
milk

(hwahng-yoh)
huángyóu
butter

Answer the *(wuhn-tee)* **wèntı** aloud.
questions

(pee-jee-oo) (zi) (nahr)
Píjiǔ zài nǎr? ....
beer   is   where

(pee-jee-oo) (zi) (beeng-ssee-ahng)(lee)
Píjiǔ zài bīngxiāng lǐ.
beer   is   refrigerator   inside

(nee-oo-ni)
Niúnǎi zài nǎr?
milk

(jee-oo)
Jiǔ zài nǎr?
wine

(hwahng-yoh)
Húangyóu zài nǎr?
butter

☐ **shǔikù** *(shwee-koo)* .... reservoir
☐ **shǔishǒu** *(shwee-shwoh)* .... sailor
☐ **shǔiyù** *(shwee-yoo)* .... body of water
☐ **shǔizai** *(shwee-zi)* .... flood
☐ **shǔiba** *(shwee-bah)* .... dam

shui

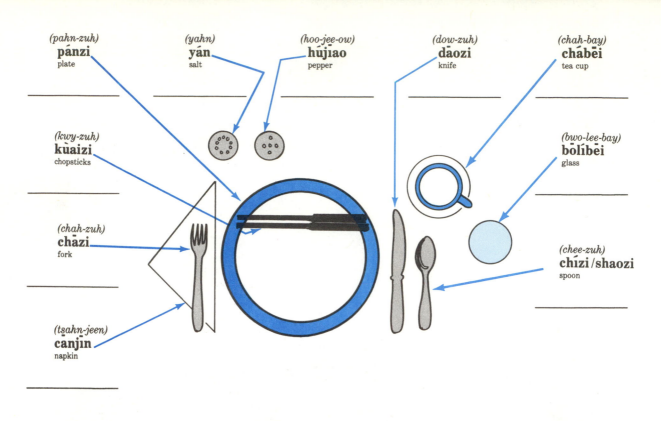

(pahn-zuh)
pánzi
plate

(yahn)
yán
salt

(hoo-jee-ow)
hújiāo
pepper

(dow-zuh)
dāozi
knife

(chah-bay)
chábēi
tea cup

(kwy-zuh)
kùaizi
chopsticks

(bwo-lee-bay)
bōlíbēi
glass

(chah-zuh)
chāzi
fork

(chee-zuh)
chízi / shaozi
spoon

(tsahn-jeen)
canjīn
napkin

(gwee-zuh)
gùizi
cupboard

(mee-ahn-bow)
miànbāo
bread

(chah)
chá
tea

(kah-fay)
kāfēi
coffee

_____   _____   *chá*   _____

(mee-ahn-bow) (zi) (nahr)
Miànbāo zài nǎr?
bread is where

Miànbāo zài gùizi
(gwee-zuh)
cupboard

(lee) (chah)
lǐ. Chá zài nǎr?
inside tea

(kah-fay)
Kāfēi zài nǎr?
coffee

(ssee-ahn-zi) (dah-ki)
Xiānzài dǎkāi
open

your **shū** with the labels and remove the next **shíjiǔ**
(shee-jee-oo)
nineteen

gè labels and proceed to label all
(guh)
(M)

these **dōngxi** in your **chúfáng.** Do not forget to use every opportunity to say these **zì**
(dwong-ssee) things   *(choo-fahng)* kitchen

out loud. **Zhè hěn zhòngyào.**
(juh) (huhn) (jwong-yow)
this very important

☐ **bīng** *(beeng)* . . . . ice
☐ **bīngbáo** *(beeng-bow)* . . . . hail
☐ **bīng diǎn** *(beeng) (dee-ahn)* . . . . freezing point
☐ **bīnglěng** *(beeng-lung)* . . . . ice-cold
☐ **bīngqílín** *(beeng-chee-leen)* . . . . ice cream

冰
bīng

There is not the wide variety of **zōngjiao** *(zwong-jee-ow)* in **Zhōngguó** *(jung-gwoh)* that **wŏmén** *(we)* find here in **Mĕigúo** *(may-gwoh)*.

In **Zhōnggúo**, a person's **zōngjiao** *(zwong-jee-ow)* **píngcháng** *(peeng-chahng)* **shi** *(shr)* one of the following.

1. **jĭdūjiao** *(jee-doo-jee-ow)* _jĭdūjiao_____
   Protestant

2. **tĭanzhŭjìao** *(tee-ahn-joo-jee-ow)* _____
   Catholic

3. **húijìao** *(hwee-jee-ow)* _____
   Moslem

4. **fojiao** *(fwo-jee-ow)* _____
   Buddist

This is a temple in **Zhōnggúo**.

You will see several **zhŭangyán** *(jwahng-yahn)* temples like *magnificent*

this on your visit. Occasionally, for special

events or for special visitors, religious

services are held in some of the temples.

Xĭanzăi *(ssee-ahn-zi)* let's learn how to say "I am" in **Zhōngwén** *(jung-wuhn)*:

I am = **wo shi**; *(woh) (shr)*
I am (in, at) = **wo zai**. *(woh)(zi)*

Practice saying "**wŏ shi**" *(woh) (shr)* and "**wŏ zài**" *(woh) (zi)* with the following **zì**. **Xĭanzăi** *(ssee-ahn-zi)* write out each

sentence for more practice.

Wŏ shi tĭanzhŭjìao tú. *(woh) (shr) (tee-ahn-joo-jee-ow)(too)* _____
I   am   Catholic   disciple

Wŏ shi jĭdūjiao tú. *(woh) (shr) (jee-doo-jee-ow)(too)* _____
I   am   Protestant   disciple

Wŏ shi húijìao tú. *(hwee-jee-ow) (too)* _____
Moslem

Wŏ shì fojiao tú. *(fwo-jee-ow)(too)* _____
Buddhist

Wŏ zài Ōuzhōu. *(oh-joh)* _Wŏ zài Ōuzhōu_
am in Europe

Wŏ zài Zhōngguo. *(jung-gwoh)* _____
am in

☐ **bingshān** *(beeng-shahn)* . . . . iceberg
☐ **bingshŭang** *(beeng-shwahng)* . . . . frost
☐ **bingtáng** *(beeng-tahng)* . . . . rock candy
☐ **bingxĭang** *(beeng-ssee-ahng)* . . . . refrigerator
☐ **bingzhŭ** *(beeng-joo)* . . . . icicle

氷
bing

35

(woh) (zi) (jee-ow-tahng)(lee)
Wǒ zài jiaotáng li. _____
I am church inside

(woh) (zi) (choo-fahng) (lee)
Wǒ zai chúfang li. _____
I am kitchen inside

(woh) (shr) (moo-cheen)
Wǒ shì muqin. _____
I am mother

(woh) (shr) (foo-cheen)
Wǒ shì fuqin. _____
I am father

(lew-gwahn)(lee)
Wǒ zài lüguan li. _____
hotel inside

(fahn-gwar) (lee)
Wǒ zài fanguar li. _____
restaurant inside

(zoo-moo)
Wǒ shì zǔmu. _____
grandmother

(zoo-foo)
Wǒ shì zǔfu. _____
grandfather

(ssee-ahn-zi) *(ruhn)* *(hwar)* *(jung-choo-eh)*
Xianzai identify all the **rén** in the **huar** below by writing the **zhengqùe** **Zhōngguó** **zì** for
person picture correct Chinese word

(ruhn) *(hwar)*
each **rén** on the line with the corresponding number under the **huar.**
person picture

1. _____   2. _____

3. _____   4. _____

5. *shūshu*   6. _____

7. _____

☐ **fēi** *(fay)* . . . . to fly
☐ **fēijī** *(fay-jee)* . . . . airplane
☐ **fēijīchǎng** *(fay-jee-chahng)* . . . . airport
☐ **fēijīkù** *(fay-jee-koo)* . . . . hangar
☐ **fēiqín** *(fay-cheen)* . . . . bird

_____
_____
飞 _____
fei _____
_____

(ssee-yoo-eh-ssee)
Xúexí
learn

Step 11

You have already used the verbs **yǒu,** *(yoh)* **xiǎng** *(ssee-ahng-yow)* **yáo,** *(yow)* **zǒu,** *(zoh)* **lái,** *(li)* **shì** *(shr)* and **zuò.** *(zwoh)* Although you
have   would like   walk   come   be   do

might be able to "get by" with these verbs, let's assume you want to do better than that.

First, a quick review.

In **Zhōngwén,** how do you say 「"I"」 In **Zhōngwén,** how do you say 「"we"」 ? _____

Compare zhè *(juh)* **liǎng** *(lee-ahng)* **ge** *(guh)* charts
these   two   (M)

hěn *(huhn)* carefully and **xúexí** *(ssee-yoo-eh-ssee)*
very   learn

zhè *(juh)* **lìu** *(lee-oo)* **gè** *(guh)* **zì** *(zuh)* on the right.
these   six   (M)   words

I =	**wǒ** *(woh)*
you =	**nǐ** *(nee)*
he =	**tā** *(tah)*
she =	**tā** *(tah)*
it =	**tā** *(tah)*

we =	**wǒmén** *(woh-muhn)*
they =	**tāmén** *(tah-muhn)*

Xìanzài draw lines between the matching **Yīngwén** *(yeeng-wuhn)* and **Zhōngwén** *(jung-wuhn)* **zì** *(zuh)* below to see if you can
English   Chinese   words

keep these **zì** *(zuh)* straight in your mind.
words

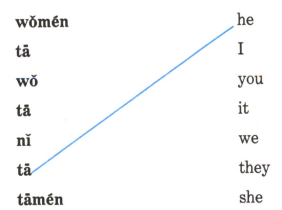

wǒmén — he

tā — I

wǒ — you

tā — it

nǐ — we

tā — they

tāmén — she

Xìanzài close this **shū** and write out both columns of the above practice on a piece of **zhǐ.** *(juhr)*
paper

How did **nǐ** *(nee)* do? **Hǎo,** *(how)* or **bùhǎo?** *(boo-how)* **Māmǎhūhū?** *(mah-mah-hoo-hoo)* **Xìanzài** that **nǐ** *(nee)* know these **zì,** *(zuh)* **nǐ** *(nee)* can say
you   good   no good   so so   words

almost anything in **Zhōngwén** with one basic formula: the "plug-in" formula. With this

formula, you can correctly use any **zì** *(zuh)* **nǐ** *(nee)* wish.
words you

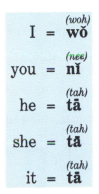

☐ **fēisù** *(fay-soo)*	quickly	
☐ **fēiwǔ** *(fay-woo)*	to flutter	*fei*
☐ **fēixíng** *(fay-sseeng)*	to soar	
☐ **fēixíngyúan** *(fay-sseeng-yoo-ahn)*	pilot	
☐ **fēiyú** *(fay-yoo)*	flying fish	

37

To demonstrate, let's take **liù** *(lee-oo)* (six) **gè** *(guh)* (M) basic and practical verbs and see how the "plug-in"

formula works. Write the verbs in the blanks below after **nǐ** have practiced saying them.

lái *(li)* = to come   **qù** *(chee-oo)* = to go   **xúexí** *(ssee-yoo-eh-ssee)* = to learn

lái
_____   _____   _____

xūyào *(ssee-oo-yow)* = to need   **yǒu** *(yoh)* = to have   **xiǎng yào** *(ssee-ahng)(yow)* = would like

_____   _____   _____

Study the following verb patterns carefully.

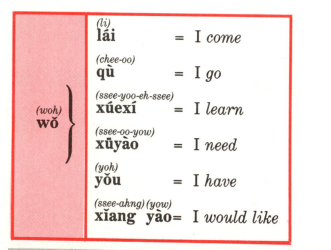

wǒ *(woh)*	**lái** *(li)*	= I *come*
	qù *(chee-oo)*	= I *go*
	xúexí *(ssee-yoo-eh-ssee)*	= I *learn*
	xūyào *(ssee-oo-yow)*	= I *need*
	yǒu *(yoh)*	= I *have*
	xiǎng yào *(ssee-ahng) (yow)*	= I *would like*

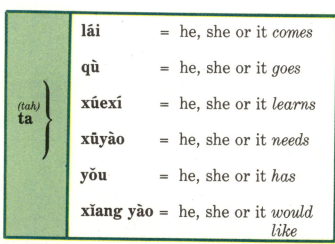

ta *(tah)*	**lái**	= he, she or it *comes*
	qù	= he, she or it *goes*
	xúexí	= he, she or it *learns*
	xūyào	= he, she or it *needs*
	yǒu	= he, she or it *has*
	xiǎng yào	= he, she or it *would like*

Note: • Whether you are speaking about "I," "he," "she," "it," "they," or "we,"

the same verb form is used. Verbs remain the same in Chinese—

they do not have different endings.

ex. **wǒ yǒu** *(yoh)*   *ex.* **wǒ lái** *(li)*

nǐ yǒu   **nǐ lái**

tā yǒu   **tā lái**

wǒmén yǒu   **wǒmén lái**

tāmén yǒu   **tāmén lái**

☐ **shū** *(shoo)* .... book
☐ **shūbāo** *(shoo-bow)* .... bookbag
☐ **shūchú** *(shoo-choo)* .... bookcase
☐ **shūjià** *(shoo-jee-ah)* .... bookshelf
☐ **shūqiān** *(shoo-chee-ahn)* .... bookmark

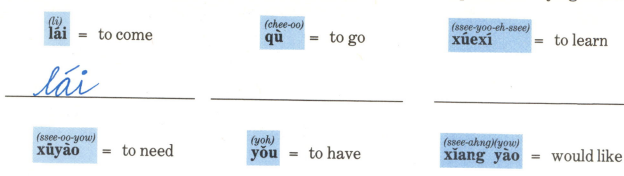 *shu*
_____
_____
_____
_____

Again, notice that **wǒmèn** *(woh-muhn)* and **tāmèn** *(tah-muhn)* use the same verb form as **wǒ** *(woh)*, **nǐ** *(nee)* and **tā** *(tah)*.
we   they   I   you   he, she, it

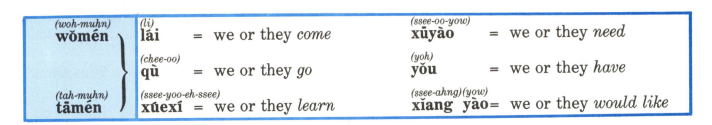

(woh-muhn) **wǒmèn**	*(li)* **lái**	= we or they *come*	*(ssee-oo-yow)* **xūyào**	= we or they *need*
	(chee-oo) **qù**	= we or they *go*	*(yoh)* **yǒu**	= we or they *have*
(tah-muhn) **tāmèn**	*(ssee-yoo-eh-ssee)* **xúexí**	= we or they *learn*	*(ssee-ahng)(yow)* **xǐang yào**	= we or they *would like*

Note: • Unlike English, the same word is used for he, she and it: **tā.** *(tah)*

• "**mén**" *(muhn)* is added to a word to indicate more than one person, as in **wǒmén** *(woh-muhn)*
we

and **tāmén.** *(tah-muhn)*
they

In **Zhōngwén**, **dòngcí** *(dwong-ts)* are easy to learn. Fill in the following blanks with the **dòngcí** *(dwong-ts)*
verbs   verb

shown. Each time **nǐ** write out the sentence, be sure to say it aloud. At the back of this

shū, nǐ will also find flash cards that will help **nǐ** to learn these new **dòngcí.** Cut them out,

carry them in your briefcase, purse, pocket or knapsack, and review them whenever **nǐ**

have a free moment.

(ssee-yoo-eh-ssee)
xúexí
learn

(woh)
Wǒ _____ **Zhōngwén.**
I

(nee)
Nǐ _____ **Yīngwén.** *(yeeng-wuhn)*
you   English

(tah)
Tā _____ **Zhōngwén.**
he, she, it

(woh-muhn)
Wǒmén _____*xúexí*_____ **Yīngwén.** *(yeeng-wuhn)*
we   English

(tah-muhn)
Tāmén _____ **Zhōngwén.**
they

(li)
lái
come

Wǒ _____ **Měiguó.** *(may-gwoh)*
America

Nǐ _____*lái*_____ **Déguó.** *(duh-gwoh)*
Germany

Tā _____ **Fǎguó.** *(fah-gwoh)*
France

Wǒmén _____ **Yīngguó.** *(yeeng-gwoh)*
England

Tāmén _____ **Zhōngguó.**

39

(chee-oo)
qù
go

(woh)
Wǒ _____ **Déguo.**
I   Germany *(duh-gwoh)*

(nee)
Nǐ _____ *qù* _____ **Fǎguo.**
you   France *(fah-gwoh)*

(tah)
Tā _____ **Yìdàlì.**
he, she, it   Italy *(yee-dah-lee)*

(woh-muhn)
Wǒmén _____ **Hélán.**
we   Netherlands *(huh-lahn)*

(tah-muhn)
Tāmén _____ **Zhōngguo.**
they

(ssee-oo-yow)
xūyào
need

(yee) (jee-ahn) (woo-zuh)
Wǒ _____ **yì jiān wūzi.**
one (M)   room

Nǐ _____ **yì jiān wūzi.**
one (M)   room *(yee) (jee-ahn) (woo-zuh)*

Tā _____ *xūyào* _____ **yì jiān wūzi.**

Wǒmén _____ **yì jiān wūzi.**

Tāmén _____ **yì jiān wūzi.**

(yoh)
you
have

(ssee-ahng) (yow)
xiǎng yào
would like

(woo) (yoo-ahn)
Wǒ _____ *yǒu* _____ **wǔ yúan.**
five   yuan

(lee-oo) (yoo-ahn)
Nǐ _____ **lìu yúan.**
six   yuan

(bah)
Tā _____ **bā yúan.**
eight

(shr)
Wǒmén _____ **shí yúan.**
ten

(sahn)
Tāmén _____ **sān yúan.**
three

(yee) (bay) (jee-oo)
Wǒ _____ **yì bēi jǐu.**
cup, glass   wine

(yee) (bay) (chah)
Nǐ _____ **yì bēi chá.**
cup   tea

(bay) (shwee)
Tā _____ **yì bēi shǔi.**
glass   water

(joo-zuh-shwee)
Wǒmén _____ **yì bēi júzishǔi.**
orange juice

Tāmén _____ *xiǎng yào* _____ **yì bēi píjǐu.**
beer *(pee-jee-oo)*

(juhr) (yoh) (lee-oo) (guh) (dwong-ts)
Zhěr yǒu lìu ge dòngcí.
here are six (M) verbs

(jee-ow)
jiao = to be called

(my)
mǎi = to buy

(shwoh)
shūo = to speak

_____

_____

_____

(joo)
zhù = to live/reside

(jee-ow)
jiao = to order

(teeng-lee-oo)
tínglíu = to stay

_____

_____

_____

40

Xìanzài fill in the following blanks with the correct form of each verb. Be sure to say each sentence out loud until **nǐ** have it down pat!

(jee-ow)
jìao
be called

Wǒ _jìao_ *(yoo-eh-hahn)* **Jūehàn.**
John

Nǐ _____ *(mah-lee)* **Mǎlì.**
Mary

Tā _____ **Jìan.**

Wǒmén _____ Jūehàn, Mǎlì hé Jìan. *(huh)*
and

Tāmén _____ Jūehàn, Mǎlì hé Jìan. *(huh)*
and

(my)
mǎi
buy

Wǒ _____ yī lǐang zìxíngchē. *(yee)* *(zuh-sseeng-chuh)*
one (M) bicycle

Nǐ _____ yí gè sǎlà. *(guh)(sah-lah)*
(M) salad

Tā _____ yī zhǎng hùar. *(jahng)(hwar)*
(M) picture

Wǒmén _mǎi_ yí gè zhōng. *(jung)*
(M) clock

Tāmén _____ yí gè táiděng. *(ti-dung)*
(M) lamp

(shwoh)
shūo
speak

Wǒ _____ Zhōngwén.

Nǐ _shūo_ Fǎwén. *(fah-wuhn)*
French

Tā _____ Yīngwén. *(yeeng-wuhn)*
English

Wǒmén _____ Rìwén. *(ree-wuhn)*
Japanese

Tāmén _____ Déwén. *(duh-wuhn)*
German

(joo)
zhù
live/reside

Wǒ _____ zài Zhōnggúo. *(zi)*
in

Nǐ _____ zài Fǎgúo. *(zi)(fah-gwoh)*
in France

Tā _____ zài Měigúo. *(may-gwoh)*
America

Wǒmén _____ zài Ōuzhōu. *(oh-joh)*
Europe

Tāmén _zhù_ zài Dégúo. *(duh-gwoh)*
Germany

(jee-ow)
jìao
order

Wǒ _____ yì bēi shǔi. *(bay)(shwee)*
glass water

Nǐ _____ yì bēi jǐu. *(jee-oo)*
wine

Tā _jìao_ yì bēi júzishǔi. *(joo-zuh-shwee)*
orange juice

Wǒmén _____ yì bēi chá.

Tāmén _____ yì bēi níunǎi. *(nee-oo-ni)*
milk

(teeng-lee-oo)
tínglíu
stay

Wǒ _____ wǔ tīan. *(woo)(tee-ahn)*
five days

Nǐ _tínglíu_ sǎn tīan. *(sahn)(tee-ahn)*
three days

Tā _____ lǐang tīan. *(lee-ahng)*
two

Wǒmén _____ lìu tīan. *(lee-oo)*
six

Tāmén _____ bā tīan. *(bah)*
eight

41

Xìanzài see if **nǐ** can fill in the blanks below. The correct answers *(zi)* **zǎi** the bottom of are at

(juh-ay)(yeh)
zhèi yě.
this   page

1. I speak Chinese. _____

2. He comes from America. _____

3. We learn Chinese. _____

4. They have 10 yuan. _____

5. She would like one glass of water. _____

6. We need one room. _____

7. I am called Mary. _____

8. I live in America. _____

9. You are buying one book. *Nǐ mǎi yì běn shū.*

10. He orders one beer. _____

In the following Steps, **nǐ** will be introduced to more and more *(dwong-ts)* **dòngcí** and **nǐ** should
                                                                          verbs

drill them in exactly the same way as **nǐ** did in this section. Look up *(sseen)* **xīn zì** in your
                                                                                       new

(zuh) (dee-ahn)
zì diǎn and make up your own sentences using the same type of pattern. Remember, the
dictionary

more **nǐ** practice, the more enjoyable your trip will be. Good luck!

Be sure to check off your fun **zì** in the box provided as **nǐ** learn each one.

(fuhn)
Fēn
minutes

Nǐ know **zěnme** to tell the **tiān** of the **xīngqī** and the **yùe** of the **nián**, so **xiànzài** let's
(how) (days) (week) (months) (year) (zuhn-muh) (sseeng-chee) (yoo-eh) (nee-ahn)

learn to tell time. Punctuality **zài Zhōngguó hěn zhòngyào**, not to mention the need of
(in) (very) (important) (zi) (huhn) (jwong-yow)

catching **huǒchē** and arriving on time. **Zhèr shì** the "basics." Notice that **le**, like
(trains) (here) (are) (hwoh-chuh) (juhr) (shr)

ma, is often used to complete sentences and words in **Zhōngwén**.

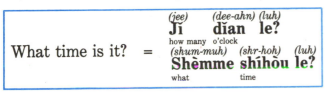

What time is it? =	(jee) (dee-ahn) (luh) **Jǐ diǎn le?** how many o'clock (shum-muh) (shr-hoh) (luh) **Shěmme shíhòu le?** what time

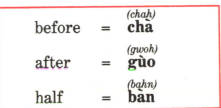

before = **chà** (chah)

after = **gùo** (gwoh)

half = **bàn** (bahn)

(dee-ahn)
Wǔ diǎn.
five o'clock

(dee-ahn) (bahn)
Sì diǎn bàn.
four o'clock half

Sān diǎn.

(bahn)
Liǎng diǎn bàn.
half

Bā diǎn èrshí fēn.
eight o'clock twenty minutes
(fuhn)

OR

Bā diǎn gùo èrshí fēn.
after twenty minutes
(gwoh) (fuhn)

Qī diǎn sìshí fēn.
o'clock minutes
(dee-ahn) (fuhn)

OR

Chà èrshí fēn bā diǎn.
before
(chah)

Xiànzài fill in the blanks according to the **shíjiān** indicated on the **zhǒng**.
(shr-jee-ahn) time (jung)

The answers **zài** below. Remember that **liǎng** means two in **Zhōngwén**, as does **èr**.
(are) (lee-ahng) (ur)

sì diǎn

(juhr)
Zhèr are more time-telling **zì** to add to your **zì** power.
here

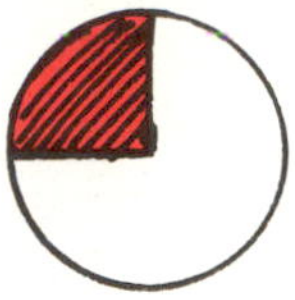

(yee) (kuh) **yí kè**	=	one quarter
(chah) (kuh) **chà yí kè**	=	one quarter before
(gwoh) (kuh) **gùo yí kè**	=	one quarter after

Lǐang (dee-ahn) **dǐan** (o'clock) **yí** (one) (kuh) **kè.** (quarter) OR **Lǐang dǐan shíwǔ** (fuhn) **fēn.** (minutes)

Chà yí (kuh) **kè lǐang dǐan.** OR **Yì dǐan sìshíwǔ fēn.**

Xìanzài it is your turn.

__________________________. __________________________.

chà yí kè sān dǐan. __________________________.

See how (jwong-yow) **zhōngyào** (important) learning (shoo-zuh) **shùzì** (numbers) is? **Xìanzài** answer the following (wuhn-tee) **wèntí** (questions) based on the **zhōng** below. The answers **zài** the bottom of (juh-ay) **zhèi** (this) **yè.**

Jǐ dǐan le?

1 

2 

3 

4 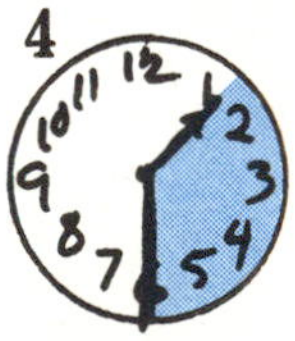

5 

6 

7 

1. lìu dǐan
2. ______________________________
3. ______________________________
4. ______________________________
5. ______________________________
6. ______________________________
7. ______________________________

ANSWERS

1. lìu dǐan
2. qī dǐan bàn (qī dǐan sānshí fēn)
3. bā dǐan
4. yì dǐan bàn (yì dǐan sānshí fēn)
5. shíer dǐan yí kè (shíer dǐan shíwǔ fēn)
6. jǐu dǐan èrshí (fēn) (jǐu dǐan gùo èrshí fēn)
7. lǐang dǐan yí kè (lǐang dǐan gùo yí kè)

When **nǐ** answer a **shíjiān** *(shr-jee-ahn)* **wèntí** *(wuhn-tee)*, it is not necessary to say **fēn** *(fuhn)* after the
time   question

number of minutes.

Huǒchē *(hwoh-chuh)* **shénme** **shíhòu** *(shr-hoh)* **lái** *(li)*? <u>*Liù diǎn*</u>.
train 火车   what   time   come

Xìanzài answer the following **wèntí** based on the **zhōng** below. Be sure to practice saying

each **wèntí** out loud several times.

Yīnyuè *(yeen-yoo-eh)* **huì** *(hwee)* **shénme** **shíhòu** *(shr-hoh)* **kāishǐ** *(ki-shr)*? _____.
music   concert what   time   start

Xìyuàn *(ssee-yoo-ahn)* **shénme** **shíhòu** **kāi** *(ki)*? _____.
theater   open

Gōnggòngqìchē *(goong-goong-chee-chuh)* **shénme** **shíhòu** **lái** *(li)*? _____.
bus   come

Chūchāichē *(choo-chi-chuh)* **shénme** **shíhòu** **lái** *(li)*? _____.
taxi   come

Fànguǎr *(fahn-gwar)* **shénme** **shíhòu** **kāi** *(ki)*? _____.
restaurant   open

Fànguǎr *(fahn-gwar)* **shénme** **shíhòu** **guānmén** *(gwahn-muhn)*? _____.
restaurant   close

Shàngwǔ bā diǎn *(dee-ahn)* **rén** *(ruhn)* **shūo** *(shwoh)*,
morning   o'clock   person says

"**Nǐ hǎo ma, Wáng tóngzhì** *(twong-juhr)*?"
how are you   comrade

Xìawǔ sān diǎn rén chángcháng *(chahng-chahng)* **shūo** *(shwoh)*,
afternoon   o'clock   often

"**Jīntian tianqì hěn hǎo!**"
today   weather   very   good

Xìawu yì diǎn rén shūo *(ssee-ah-woo)* *(shwoh)*,
afternoon   o'clock   says

"**Chī fàn le ma, tóngzhì** *(chr)* *(fahn)* *(twong-juhr)*?"
have you eaten   comrade

Wǎnshàng shí diǎn rén shūo,
evening   o'clock

"**Míngtian jìan.**"
see you   tomorrow

45

Remember:

What time is it? = **Shénme shíhóu le?** *(shun-muh) (shr-hoh) (luh)*

Jǐ dǐan le?
how many o'clock

When / at what time = **shénme shíhóu** *(shun-muh) (shr-hoh)*

Can **nǐ** pronounce and understand

the following paragraph?

15:15 **huoche cóng Shanghai lái.** *(hwoh-chuh) (shahng-hi)*

Xianzai shì 15:20. Huoche wan le. *(ssee-ahn-zi) (wahn)*
late

Jīntian huoche 17:15 lái.

Mingtian 15:15 huoche zai lái. *(meeng-tee-ahn) (zi)*
again

Zher shì more practice exercises. *(juhr) (shr)*
here

Answer **zhè xie wèntí** based on the **shíjian** given. *(juh) (ssee-eh) (shr-jee-ahn)*
these several

Jǐ dǐan le?

1. (10:30) *shí dǐan bàn*

2. (6:30) _____

3. (2:15) _____

4. (11:40) _____

5. (12:18) _____

6. (7:20) _____

7. (3:10) _____

8. (4:05) _____

9. (5:35) _____

10. (11:50) _____

☐ **fáng** *(fahng)* .... room, apartment
☐ **fángdong** *(fang-dwong)* .... landlord
☐ **fángkè** *(fahng-kuh)* .... tenant
☐ **fángzi** *(fahng-zuh)* .... house
☐ **wòfang** *(wo-fahng)* .... bedroom

房
fang

Zhèr shì yí gè quick quiz. Fill in the blanks with **zhèngquè shùzì.** The answers

(juhr) (shr) here is (M) *(jung-choo-eh)* correct

zài xiàbianr.

(ssee-bee-ahnr) under, below

1. **Yì fēn yǒu** _____ **miǎo.**
   minute has (?) seconds
   (fuhn)(yoh) *(mee-ow)*

2. **Yí gè zhōngtóu yǒu** _____ **fēn.**
   (M) hour has (?) minutes
   (jung-toh) *(yoh)* *(fuhn)*

3. **Yì tiān yǒu** _____ **zhōngtóu.**
   day (?) hours
   (tee-ahn) *(jung-toh)*

4. **Yí gè xīngqī yǒu** _qī_ **tiān.**
   week (?) days
   (sseeng-chee) *(tee-ahn)*

5. **Yí gè yuè yǒu** _____ **tiān.**
   (M) month (?) days
   (yoo-eh) *(tee-ahn)*

6. **Yì nián yǒu** _____ **gè yuè.**
   years (?) (M) months
   (nee-ahn) *(yoo-eh)*

7. **Yì nián yǒu** _____ **gè xīngqī.**
   year (?) (M) weeks
   (nee-ahn) *(sseeng-chee)*

8. **Yì nián yǒu** _____ **tiān.**
   year (?)
   (nee-ahn)

Zhèr is a sample **Zhōngguóde huǒchē shíjiān biǎo. Tèkuài shì tèbié kuàide huǒchē.**

here Chinese train time schedule express special fast
(hwoh-chuh) (shr-jee-ahn) (bee-ow) *(tuh-kwy) (tuh-bee-eh) (kwy-duh)*

Kuàichē shì kuài yìdiǎr. Pǔtōngchē shì màn chē.

fast a little ordinary train slow vehicle
(kwy-chuh) (kwy) (yee-dee-ahr)(poo-twong-chuh) (mahn) (chuh)

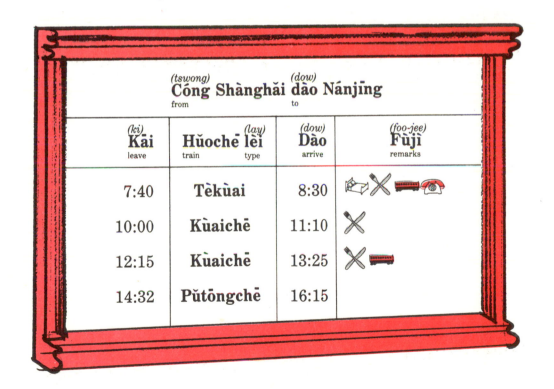

Cóng Shànghǎi dào Nánjīng			
from	to		
Kāi	**Huǒchē lèi**	**Dào**	**Fùjì**
leave *(ki)*	train type *(lay)*	arrive *(dow)*	remarks *(foo-jee)*
7:40	Tèkuài	8:30	🛏️🍴🚃☎️
10:00	Kuàichē	11:10	🍴
12:15	Kuàichē	13:25	🍴🚃
14:32	Pǔtōngchē	16:15	

47

Zhèr shì jǐ gè xīn dòngcí for Step 12.
(jee) (sseen) (dwong-ts)
here are some (M) new verbs

shūo *(shwoh)* = to say   **chī** *(chr)* = to eat   **hē** *(huh)* = to drink

_____   _____chī_____   _____

shūo *(shwoh)*
say

Wǒ jīntiān _____shūo_____.

Nǐ _____ "hǎo!" *(how)*
all right

Tā jīntiān _____ hěn dūo. *(huhn) (dwoh)*
very much

Wǒmén _____ "búyào." *(boo-yow)*
don't want it

Tāmén méi _____. *(may)*
didn't

chī *(chr)*
eat

Wǒ _____ shuǐguǒ. *(shwee-gwoh)*
fresh fruit

Nǐ _____ zǎofàn. *(zow-fahn)*
breakfast

Tā _____ yú. *(tah)* *(yoo)*
fish

Wǒmén _____ ròu. *(roh)*
meat

Tāmén _____ jīdàn. *(jee-dahn)*
eggs

hē *(huh)*
drink

Wǒ _____ niúnǎi. *(nee-oo-ni)*
milk

Nǐ _____ júzishuǐ. *(joo-zuh-shwee)*
orange juice

Tā _____hē_____ jiǔ. *(jee-oo)*
wine

Wǒmén _____ qìshuǐ. *(chee-shwee)*
pop

Tāmén _____ kěkǒukělè. *(kuh-koh-kuh-luh)*
coke

Remember that **"c"** is pronounced like the **"ts"** in its.

48

(hwar) **hùar**	*(shoo-fahng)* **shūfáng**	*(jee-oo)* **jĭu**	*(meeng-tee-ahn jee-ahn)* **Mìngtiān jìan.**
(tee-ahn-hwah-bahn) **tīanhŭabăn**	*(dee-ssee-ah-shr)* **dìxìashì**	*(shr)* **shí**	*(wahn-shahng jee-ahn)* **Wănshàng jìan.**
(chee-ahng-jee-ow) **qíangjĭao**	*(chuh-fahng)* **chēfáng**	*(bi)* **bái**	*(ssee-ah-woo jee-ahn)* **Xìawŭ jìan.**
(chwahng-hoo) **chūanghù**	*(chee-chuh)* **qìchē**	*(hay)* **hēi**	*(beeng-ssee-ahng)* **bīngxīang**
(dung) **dēng**	*(zuh-sseeng-chuh)* **zìxíngchē**	*(hwahng)* **húang**	*(loo-zuh)* **lúzi**
(ti-dung) **táidēng**	*(goh)* **gŏu**	*(hohng)* **hóng**	*(jee-oo)* **jĭu**
(shah-fah) **shāfā**	*(mow)* **māo**	*(lahn)* **lán**	*(pee-jee-oo)* **píjĭu**
(yee-zuh) **yĭzi**	*(hwah-yoo-ahn)* **hūayúan**	*(hwee)* **hūi**	*(nee-oo-ni)* **níunăi**
(dee-tahn) **dìtăn**	*(hwar)* **hūar**	*(kah-fay)* **kāfēi**	*(hwahng-yoh)* **húangyóu**
(jwoh-zuh) **zhūozi**	*(yoh-twong)* **yóutŏng**	*(lew)* **lǚ**	*(pahn-zuh)* **pánzi**
(muhn) **mén**	*(sseen)* **xìn**	*(fuhn)* **fĕn**	*(dow-zuh)* **dāozi**
(jung) **zhōng**	*(muhn-leeng)* **ménlíng**	*(hwah)* **hūa**	*(chah-zuh)* **chāzi**
(chwahng-lee-ahn) **chūanglían**	*(yee)* **yī**	*(sseeng-chee-yee)* **xīngqīyī**	*(chee-zuh)* **chízi**
(chee-ahng) **qíang**	*(ur)* **èr**	*(sseeng-chee-ur)* **xīngqìèr**	*(kwy-zuh)* **kùaizi**
(fahng-zuh) **fángzi**	*(sahn)* **sān**	*(sseeng-chee-sahn)* **xīngqīsān**	*(tsahn-jeen)* **cānjīn**
(fahn-teeng) **fàntīng**	*(see)* **sì**	*(sseeng-chee-see)* **xīngqīsì**	*(chah-bay)* **chábēi**
(kuh-teeng) **kètīng**	*(woo)* **wŭ**	*(sseeng-chee-woo)* **xīngqīwŭ**	*(bwo-lee-bay)* **bōlíbēi**
(wo-fahng) **wòfáng**	*(lee-oo)* **lìu**	*(sseeng-chee-lee-oo)* **xīngqīlìu**	*(yahn)* **yán**
(ssee-zow-fahng) **xĭzăofáng**	*(chee)* **qī**	*(sseeng-chee-tee-ahn)* **xīngqītīan**	*(hoo-jee-ow)* **hújīao**
(choo-fahng) **chúfáng**	*(bah)* **bā**	*(nee how)* **Nĭ hăo?**	*(gwee-zuh)* **gùizi**

STICKY LABELS

This book has over 150 special sticky labels for you to use as you learn new words. When you are introduced to a word, remove the corresponding label from these pages. Be sure to use each of these unique labels by adhering them to a picture, window, lamp, or whatever object it refers to.

The sticky labels make learning to speak Chinese much more fun and a lot easier than you ever expected.

For example, when you look in the mirror and see the label, say

(jeeng-zuh)
"jìngzi."

Don't just say it once, say it again and again.

And once you label the refrigerator, you should never again open that door without saying

(beeng-ssee-ahng)
"bīngxiāng."

By using the sticky labels, you not only learn new words but friends and family learn along with you!

48a

(mee-ahn-bow) **mìanbāo**	*(juhr)* **zhǐ**	*(fay-zow)* **féizào**	*(leeng-di)* **lǐngdài**
(chah) **chá**	*(zuh-juhr-loh)* **zìzhǐlǒu**	*(yah-shwah)* **yáshūa**	*(shoh-jwahn)* **shǒujùan**
(kah-fay) **kāfēi**	*(yoh-jee-ahn)* **yóujìan**	*(yah-gow)* **yágāo**	*(shahng-yee)* **shàngyī**
(shwee) **shǔi**	*(yoh-pee-ow)* **yóupìao**	*(shoo-zuh)* **shūzi**	*(koo-zuh)* **kùzi**
(joo-zuh-shwee) **júzǐshǔi**	*(shoo)* **shū**	*(wi-yee)* **wàiyī**	*(chun-yee)* **chènyī**
(chwahng) **chúang**	*(meeng-sseen-pee-ahn)* **míngxìnpìan**	*(yoo-yee)* **yǔyī**	*(chahng-yee-foo)* **chángyīfu**
(bay) **bèi**	*(zah-juhr)* **zázhì**	*(sahn)* **sǎn**	*(choon-zuh)* **qúnzi**
(juhn-toh) **zhěntóu**	*(bow-juhr)* **bàozhǐ**	*(shoh-tow)* **shǒutào**	*(mow-yee)* **máoyī**
(now-jung) **nàozhōng**	*(yahn-jeeng)* **yǎnjìng**	*(mow-zuh)* **màozi**	*(nay-koo)* **nèikù**
(yee-choo) **yīchú**	*(dee-ahn-shr)* **dìanshì**	*(ssee-eh)* **xíe**	*(nay-yee)* **nèiyī**
(ssee-lee-ahn-puhn) **xǐlǐanpén**	*(hoo-jow)* **hùzhào**	*(ssee-yoo-eh-zuh)* **xūezi**	*(chun-choon)* **chènqún**
(leen-yoo) **línyù**	*(fay-jee-pee-ow)* **fēijīpìao**	*(wah-zuh)* **wàzi**	*(ssee-wong-jow)* **xiōngzhào**
(mah-twong) **mǎtǒng**	*(chee-ahn)* **qían**	*(koo-wah)* **kùwà**	*(neen mahn-mahn chr)* **Nín mànmān chī!**
(mow-jeen) **máojīn**	*(jow-ssee-ahng-jee)* **zhàoxìangjī**	*(shwee-yee)* **shùiyī**	*(mahng)* **máng**
(ssee-ow) *(mow-jeen)* **xǐao máojīn**	*(dee-pee-ahn)* **dǐpìan**	*(twoh-ssee-eh)* **tūoxíe**	*(dwee-boo-chee)* **dùibùqǐ**
(ssee-zow) *(mow-jeen)* **xǐzǎo máojīn**	*(ssee-ahng-zuh)* **xìangzi**	*(shwee-pow)* **shùipáo**	*(cheeng)* **qǐng**
(ssee-lee-ahn) *(mow-jeen)* **xǐlǐan máojīn**	*(pee-jee-ah-zuh)* **píjīazi**	*(ssee-jwahng)* **xīzhūang**	*(ssee-eh-ssee-eh)* **xìexìe**
(jeeng-zuh) **jìngzi**	*(pee-bow)* **píbāo**	*(woh shr may-gwoh-ruhn)* **Wǒ shì Měigúorén.**	
(chee-ahn-bee) **qīanbǐ**	*(yoh-yong-yee)* **yóuyǒngyī**	*(woh ssee-ahng yow ssee-yoo-eh-ssee jung-wuhn)* **Wǒ xǐang yào xúexí Zhōngwén.**	
(gahng-bee) **gāngbǐ**	*(lee-ahng-ssee-eh)* **líangxíe**	*(woh jee-ow)* **Wǒ jìao _____.**	

PLUS . . .

Your book includes a number of other innovative features. At the back of the book, you'll find seven pages of flash cards. Cut them out and flip through them at least once a day.

On pages 112 and 113, you'll find a beverage guide and a menu guide. Don't wait until your trip to use them. Clip out the menu guide and use it tonight at the dinner table. And use the beverage guide to practice ordering your favorite drinks.

By using the special features in this book, you will be speaking Chinese before you know it.

(yee) (loo) (peeng) (ahn)
Yí lù píng ān!
safe and peaceful journey

(dwong) *(nahn)* *(ssee)* *(bay)*
Dōng - Nán, Xī - Běi
east   south   west   north

Step 13

While in **Zhōngguó, nǐ** *(nee)* will probably use a **dìtú** *(dee-too)* to find your way around. Study the
you   map

direction words **xiàbianr** *(ssee-ah-bee-ahnr)* until **nǐ** are familiar with them and can recognize them on
below

your **dìtú** *(dee-too)* of **Zhōngguó.**
map

(dwong) **dōng** east	*(nahn)* **nán** south	*(ssee)* **xī** west	*(bay)* **bēi** north

Notice on your **dìtú** *(dee-too)* how directions in **Zhōngguó** are given as eastsouth **dōngnán** and westnorth **xībēi**,
map

rather than southeast and northwest. Also notice how the direction words, **dōng** *(dwong)*, **nán** *(nahn)*,
east   south

xī *(ssee)*, and **bēi** *(bay)* are used below with the words **bianr** *(bee-ahnr)*, meaning side and **fāng** *(fahng)*, meaning direction.
west   north

(dwong-bee-ahnr) **dōngbianr**	=	the east _____
(nahn-bee-ahnr) **nánbianr**	=	the south _____
(ssee-bee-ahnr) **xībianr**	=	the west *xībianr*
(bay-bee-ahnr) **běibianr**	=	the north _____

(dwong-fahng) **dōngfāng**	=	eastern _____
(nahn-fahng) **nánfāng**	=	southern *nánfāng*
(ssee-fahng) **xifāng**	=	western _____
(bay-fahng) **běifāng**	=	northern _____

In **Zhōngwén, xīyáng** *(ssee-yahng)*, meaning West Ocean, refers to any western country, like the

United States, England or Germany. **Dōngyáng** *(dwong-yahng)*, meaning East Ocean, refers to Japan.

But what about more basic directions such as "left," "right," "straight ahead" and "around

the corner"? Let's **xiànzài** learn these **zì.**
now

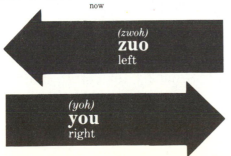

(zwoh) **zuo** left

(yoh) **you** right

straight ahead	=	**yìzhí** *(yee-juhr)* **zōu** *(zwoh)* straight walk
around the corner	=	**zhǔan** *(juh-ahn)* **jiao** *(jee-ow)* turn corner
on the right side	=	**zài** *(zi)* **yòubianr** *(yoh-bee-ahnr)* right side
on the left side	=	**zài** *(zi)* **zǔobianr** *(zwoh-bee-ahnr)* left side

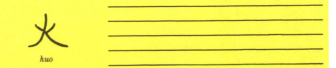

☐ **hǔo** *(hwoh)*	fire, flame	
☐ **hǔochái** *(hwoh-chi)*	match	
☐ **hǔojiǔ** *(hwoh-jee-oo)*	alcohol	
☐ **hǔoshān** *(hwoh-shahn)*	volcano	
☐ **hǔoyóu** *(hwoh-yoh)*	kerosene	

huo

49

Just as in **Yīngwén** *(yeeng-wuhn)* English, **sān gè zì** *(sahn)* three *(M)* go a long way.

qǐng *(cheeng)*	=	please _____
xièxie *(ssee-eh-ssee-eh)*	=	thank you *xièxie* _____
dùibùqǐ *(dwee-boo-chee)*	=	excuse me _____

Zhèr *(juhr)* here **shì** *(shr)* are **liǎng gè** two *(M)* **hěn** *(huhn)* very **diǎnxíngde** *(dee-ahn-sseeng-duh)* typical **dùihùa** *(dwee-hwah)* conversations for someone who is trying to find something.

Zhāng sān: **Dùibùqǐ.** *(dwee-boo-chee)* excuse me **Běijīng** *(bay-jeeng)* Peking **Lǚguǎn** *(lew-gwahn)* hotel **zài** *(zi)* is **nǎr?** *(nahr)* where

Lǐ sì: **Zài** *(zi)* at **qiánbianrde** *(chee-ahn-bee-ahnr-duh)* front side **jìaotáng,** *(jee-ow-tahng)* church **zǔo zhuǎn.** *(zwoh)(juh-ahn)* left turn **Zài** *(zi)* at **zǔobīanr,** *(zwoh-bee-ahnr)* left side **nǐ kànjìan** *(kahn-jee-ahn)* you see **yí gè** *(M)* **húang** *(hwahng)* yellow **fángzi** house **nà** that **shì** is **Běijīng Lǚguǎn.**

Zhāng sān: **Dùibùqǐ.** *(dwee-boo-chee)* excuse me **Zhōnggúo** Chinese **Bówùguan** *(bwo-woo-gwahn)* museum **zài nǎr?** is where

Lǐ sì: **Nǐ kànjìan** *(kahn-jee-ahn)* you see **nà gè** that *(M)* **hóng** *(hohng)* red **qìchē** *(chee-chuh)* car **ma? Zài qìchē** at car **qiánbianr,** *(chee-ahn-bee-ahnr)* front side **yòu** *(yoh)* right **zhuǎn.** *(juh-ahn)* turn **Nà jīe** *(jee-eh)* that street **shang,** *(shahng)* on **yòu** *(yoh)* has **yí gè** one *(M)* **fànguar.** *(fahn-gwar)* restaurant **Bówùguan** *(bwo-woo-gwahn)* museum **zài** is **fànguǎrde** restaurant's **yòubīanr.** *(yoh-bee-ahnr)* right side

Are you lost? There is no need to be lost if **nǐ xúexí le** *(ssee-yoo-eh-ssee)* learned the basic direction **zì.** Do not try to memorize these **dùihùa** *(dwee-hwah)* conversations because you will never be looking for precisely these places. One day you might need to ask for directions to "**Tàiyáng** *(ti-yahng)* sun **Fàngǔar** *(fahn-gwar)* restaurant" or "**Lìshǐ** *(lee-shr)* history **Bówùguǎn** *(bwo-woo-gwahn)* museum" or "**Dàlù** *(dah-loo)* mainland **Lǚguǎn.** *(lew-gwahn)* hotel" Learn the key direction **zì** and be sure **nǐ** can find your destination.

What if the person responding to your **wèntí** *(wuhn-tee)* questions answers too quickly for you to understand the entire reply? If so, ask again, saying,

☐ **hūa/hūar** *(hwah/hwar)*	....	flower	花 _____
☐ **hūa dǔo** *(hwah)(dwoh)*	....	blossom	*hua* _____
☐ **hūa píng** *(hwah)(peeng)*	....	flower vase	_____
☐ **hūa qìan** *(hwah)(chee-ahn)*	....	wreath	_____
☐ **hūa shù** *(hwah)(shoo)*	....	bouquet	_____

Xìanzài when the directions are repeated, **nǐ** will be able to understand them if **nǐ** learned

the key **zì** for directions. Quiz yourself by filling in the blanks below with the correct

Zhōnggúo zì.

Jūehàn: (dwee-boo-chee) (hi-been)
Dùibùqi. Haǐbīn Fàngǔar zài nǎr?
excuse me   seashore   hotel

Mǎlì: (zi)
Zài _____ **yóutǒng,** _____ **jǔan. Nà jīe shàng yǒu hěn**
at   front side   mailbox   right   turn that street on has very

(dwoh)
dūo qìchē. Zài _____, **gōnggòngqìchē zhàn, nǐ kànjian yí gè**
many cars at   left side   bus   stop you see   one (M)

(gow-duh) (bi) (fahng-zuh)   (yoh) (hwah-yoo-ahn)
hěn gāode baí fángzi. Fángzi _____ **yǒu hūayúan.**
very tall white house   front side   has garden

Nà shì Haǐbīn Fàngǔar.
that is

(juhr) (shr) (see) (guh) (sseen)(dwong-ts)
Zhèr shì sì gè xīn dòngcí.
here are four (M) new verbs

(jahn)
zhàn = to stand   _____

(dwong)
dǒng = to understand   *dǒng, dǒng, dǒng*

(my)
mai = to sell   _____

(zì) (shwoh)
zài shūo = to say again   _____
again speak

51

As always, say each sentence out loud. Say each and every **zì** carefully, pronouncing everything **nǐ** see.

(jahn)
zhàn
stand

Wǒ zhàn **zài** *(zi)* **zǔobīanr.** *(zwoh-bee-ahnr)* left side

Nǐ ______ **zài yòubīanr.** *(yoh-bee-ahnr)* right side

Tā ______ **zài** *(zi)* at **fángzi** *(fahng-zuh)* home **hòubīanr.** *(hoh-bee-ahnr)* behind

Wǒmén ______ **zài fángzi qíanbīanr.** *(chee-ahn-bee-ahnr)* in front of

Tāmén ______ **zài fángzi pángbīanr.** *(pahng-bee-ahnr)* next to

(dwong)
dǒng
understand

Wǒ ______ **Zhōngwén.**

Nǐ dǒng **Yīngwén.** *(yeeng-wuhn)* English

Tā ______ **Fǎwén.** *(fah-wuhn)* French

Wǒmén ______ **Déwén.** *(duh-wuhn)* German

Tāmén ______ **Rìwén.** *(ree-wuhn)* Japanese

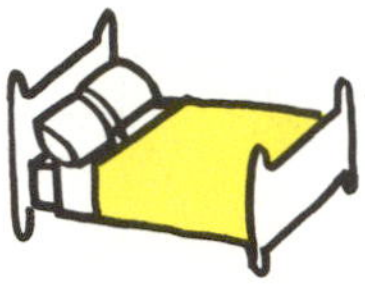

(mi)
mǎi
sell

Wǒ ______ **chúang.** *(chwahng)* bed

Nǐ ______ **hǎo** *(how)* good **yú.** *(yoo)* fish

Tā mǎi **lǜ** *(lew)* green **shàngyī.** *(shahng-yee)* jacket

Wǒmén ______ **xīn** *(sseen)* new **dìpìan.** *(dee-pee-ahn)* film

Tāmén ______ **xìpìao.** *(ssee-pee-ow)* theater tickets

(zi) *(shwoh)*
zai shuo
say again

Wǒ ______ **zhè** *(juh)* this **gè** *(guh)* (M) **zì.** *(zuh)* word

Nǐ bù *(boo)* not ______.

Tā bù *(boo)* not ______ **nà** *(nah)* that **gè** *(guh)* (M) **zì.**

Wǒmén ______.

Tāmén bù *(boo)* not zài shūo.

Xìanzài, see if **nǐ** can translate the following thoughts into **Zhōngwén.** The answers **zài xìabīanr.** *(ssee-ahn-bee-ahnr)* below

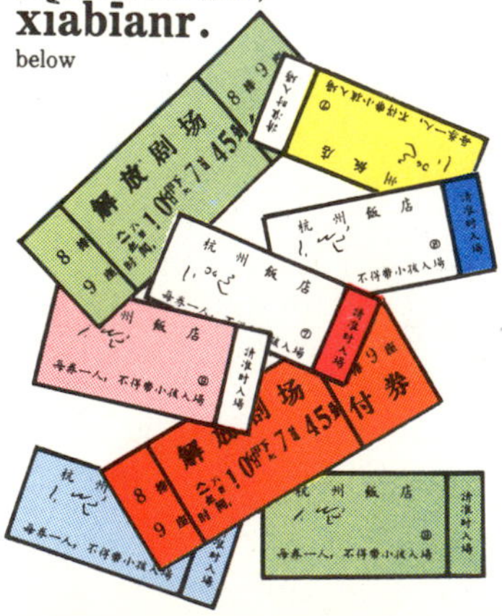

1. She again says the word. ______
2. They sell theater tickets. Tāmén mǎi xìpìao.
3. He stands in front of the house. ______
4. We eat fish. ______
5. I speak Chinese. ______
6. I drink tea. ______

ANSWERS

1. **Tā zài shuō zhè gè zì.**
2. **Tāmen mài xìpiào.**
3. **Tā zhàn zài fángzi qiánbianr.**
4. **Wǒmen chī yú.**
5. **Wǒ shuō Zhōngwén.**
6. **Wǒ hē chá.**

(shahng-bee-ahnr) *(ssee-ah-bee-ahnr)*

Shàngbianr, Xiàbianr

over, above   under, below

Before nǐ *(ki-shr)* kāishǐ Step 14, review Step 8. Xiànzài wǒmén duō xuéxí *(dwoh)* *(ssee-yoo-eh-ssee)* *(jee)* *(guh)* jǐ ge zì.
— more learn — several (M)

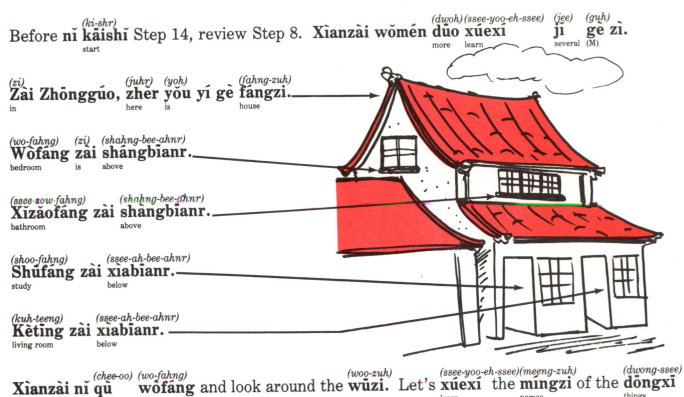

(zi) Zài Zhōngguó, zhèr yǒu yí gè fángzi. *(juhr)* *(yoh)* *(fahng-zuh)*
in — here is — house

(wo-fahng) *(zi)* *(shahng-bee-ahnr)* Wǒfáng zai shàngbianr.
bedroom — is — above

(ssee-zow-fahng) *(shahng-bee-ahnr)* Xǐzǎofáng zài shàngbianr.
bathroom — above

(shoo-fahng) *(ssee-ah-bee-ahnr)* Shūfáng zài xiàbianr.
study — below

(kuh-teeng) *(ssee-ah-bee-ahnr)* Kètīng zài xiàbianr.
living room — below

Xiànzài nǐ qù *(chee-oo)* *(wo-fahng)* wǒfáng and look around the wūzi. *(woo-zuh)* Let's xuéxí *(ssee-yoo-eh-ssee)* the míngzi *(meeng-zuh)* of the dōngxī *(dwong-ssee)*
— go bedroom — room — learn — names — things

in the wǒfáng, *(wo-fahng)* just like wǒmén xuéxí *(ssee-yoo-eh-ssee)* the various parts of the fángzi. *(fahng-zuh)* Be sure to practice
bedroom — learned — house

saying the zì as you xiě *(ssee-eh)* the míngzi *(meeng-zuh)* of these dōngxī *(dwong-ssee)* in the spaces xiàbianr. *(ssee-ah-bee-ahnr)* Also say
— write names things — below

out loud the example sentences under the hùar.

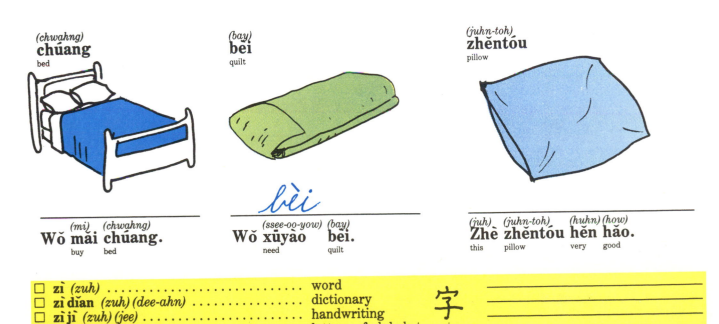

(chwahng) **chúang**
bed

Wǒ mǎi chúang. *(mi)* *(chwahng)*
— buy bed

(bay) **bèi**
quilt

bèi

Wǒ xūyào bei. *(ssee-oo-yow)* *(bay)*
— need quilt

(juhn-toh) **zhěntóu**
pillow

Zhè zhěntóu hěn hǎo. *(juh)* *(juhn-toh)* *(huhn)* *(how)*
this pillow very good

☐ zì *(zuh)*	....	word	
☐ zì dǐan *(zuh)* *(dee-ahn)*	....	dictionary	字
☐ zì jǐ *(zuh)* *(jee)*	....	handwriting	*zi*
☐ zì mǔ *(zuh)* *(moo)*	....	letters of alphabet	
☐ zì yǎn *(zuh)* *(yahn)*	....	phrase	

(now-jung)
nàozhōng
alarm clock

(yee-choo)
yīchú
clothes closet

Remove the next **wŭ** *(woo)* **gè** *(guh)* stickers
five (M)

and label these **dōngxī** *(dwong-ssee)*
things

in your **wòfáng.** *(wo-fahng)*
bedroom

(woh) (yoh) (yee) (guh)
Wŏ yŏu yí gè
I have one (M)

(now-jung)
nàozhōng.
alarm clock

(juh) (guh) (yee-choo) (zi)
Zhè gè yīchú zài
this (M) clothes closet is in

(wo-fahng)
wòfáng.
bedroom

Zài Zhōngguó, yí gè lüguănde wòfáng. *(lew-gwahn-duh)*
in   one (M) hotel's   bedroom

wò *(woh)* = to lie down (to sleep), so a sleeping room

Study the following **wèntí** *(wuhn-tee)* and their answers

based on the **zuŏbīanr hùar.** *(zwoh-bee-ahnr)*
left

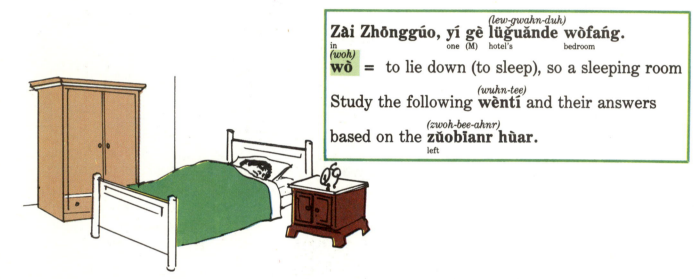

---

1. **Nàozhōng zài năr?** *(now-jung) (zi) (nahr)*
   alarm clock is where

   Nàozhōng zài zhŭozi shàng. *(jwoh-zuh) (shahng)*
   table on

2. **Bèi zài năr?** *(bay)*
   quilt

   Bèi zài chúang shàng. *(chwahng) (shahng)*
   bed on

3. **Yīchú zài năr?** *(yee-choo)*
   clothes closet

   Yīchú zài wòfáng. *(wo-fahng)*
   is in bedroom

4. **Zhĕntóu zài năr?** *(juhn-toh) (zi) (nahr)*
   pillow is where

   Zhĕntóu zài chúang shàng. *(chwahng) (shahng)*
   bed on

5. **Chúang zài năr?** *(chwahng)*
   bed

   Chúang zài wòfáng. *(wo-fahng)*
   is in bedroom

6. **Chúang dà ma? Chúang xĭao ma?** *(chwahng) (dah) (mah) (ssee-ow)*
   bed big small

   Chúang bú dà? *(boo) (dah)*
   not big

   Chúang xĭao. *(ssee-ow)*
   small

☐ **rén** *(ruhn)* .... person
☐ **nánrén** *(nahn-ruhn)* .... man
☐ **nŭrén** *(new-ruhn)* .... woman
☐ **réngé** *(ruhn-guh)* .... personality
☐ **rénkŏu** *(ruhn-koh)* .... population

人
ren

54

Xìanzài nǐ answer **wèntí** *(wuhn-tee)* based on the previous **hùar.**
questions

Nàozhōng zài nǎr? *(now-jung)*
alarm clock

Chúang zài nǎr? *(chwahng)*
bed

Nàozhōng zài _____

_____

Let's move into the **xǐzǎofáng** *(ssee-zow-fahng)* and do the same thing.
bathroom

xǐliǎnpén *(ssee-lee-ahn-puhn)*
washbasin

línyù *(leen-yoo)*
shower

mǎtǒng *(mah-twong)*
toilet

_____

Lǚguǎnde wūzi yǒu *(lew-gwahn-duh) (woo-zuh) (yoh)*
hotel room has

yí gè xǐliǎnpén. *(ssee-lee-ahn-puhn)*
one (M) washbasin

Línyù bú zài lǚguǎn *(leen-yoo) (boo) (zi) (lew-gwahn)*
shower not in hotel

wūzi. *(woo-zuh)*
room

Mǎtǒng bú zài lǚguǎn *(mah-twong) (boo) (zi) (lew-gwahn)*
toilet not in hotel

wūzi. Mǎtǒng hé línyù *(woo-zuh) (huh)*
room toilet and shower

zài dìshàng. *(zi) (dee-shahng)*
are on floor

jìngzi *(jeeng-zuh)* _____
mirror

máojīn *(mow-jeen)* *máojīn*
towels

xǐliǎn máojīn *(ssee-lee-ahn) (mow-jeen)* _____
washcloth

xiǎo máojīn *(ssee-ow) (mow-jeen)* _____
small/hand towel

xǐzǎo máojīn *(ssee-zow) (mow-jeen)* _____
bath towel

Do not forget to remove the next **xìa** *(ssee-ah)* **qī gé** *(chee)* stickers and label these
next seven (M)

dōngxi *(dwong-ssee)* in your **xǐzǎofáng.** *(ssee-zow-fahng)*
things bathroom

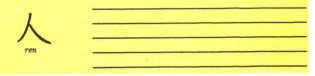

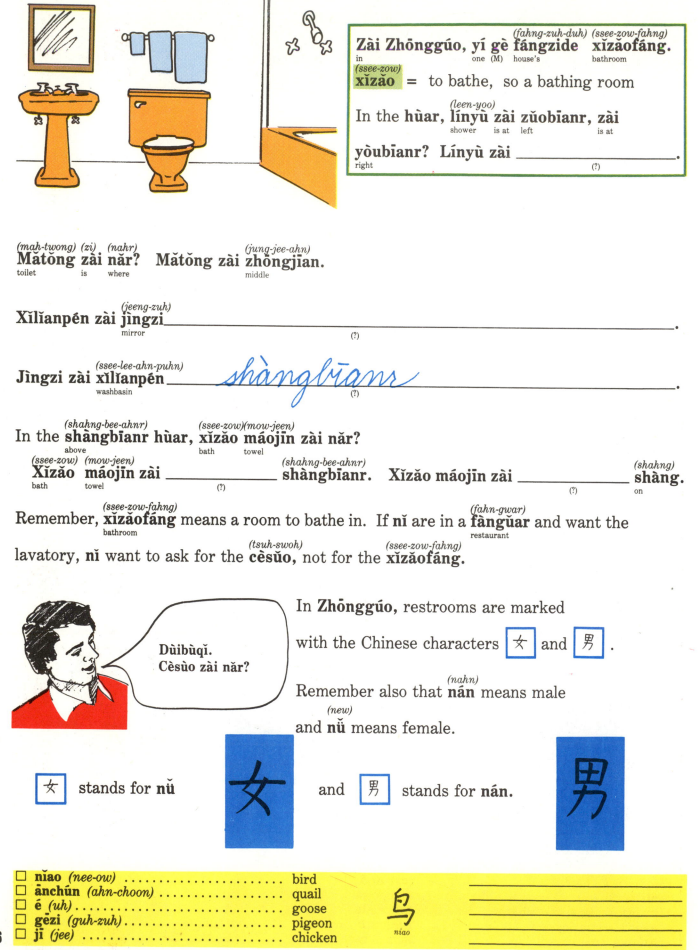

Zài Zhōnggúo, yí gè fángzide xǐzǎofáng.
(fahng-zuh-duh) *(ssee-zow-fahng)*
in   one (M) house's   bathroom

(ssee-zow)
xǐzǎo = to bathe, so a bathing room

In the **hùar, línyǔ zài zuǒbianr, zài**
(leen-yoo)
shower   is at left   is at

yòubianr? Línyù zài _____ .
right   (?)

Mǎtǒng zài nǎr? Mǎtǒng zài zhōngjīan.
(mah-twong) *(zi)* *(nahr)*   *(jung-jee-ahn)*
toilet   is   where   middle

Xǐliǎnpén zài jìngzi _____ .
(jeeng-zuh)
mirror   (?)

Jìngzi zài xǐliǎnpén _____ *shàngbīanr* _____ .
(ssee-lee-ahn-puhn)
washbasin   (?)

In the **shàngbīanr hùar, xǐzǎo máojīn zài nǎr?**
(shahng-bee-ahnr)   *(ssee-zow)(mow-jeen)*
above   bath   towel

Xǐzǎo máojīn zài _____ **shàngbīanr. Xǐzǎo máojīn zài** _____ **shàng.**
(ssee-zow) *(mow-jeen)*   (?)   *(shahng-bee-ahnr)*   (?)   *(shahng)*
bath   towel   on

Remember, **xǐzǎofáng** means a room to bathe in. If **nǐ** are in a **fàngǔar** and want the
(ssee-zow-fahng)   *(fahn-gwar)*
bathroom   restaurant

lavatory, **nǐ** want to ask for the **cèsǔo,** not for the **xǐzǎofáng.**
(tsuh-swoh)   *(ssee-zow-fahng)*

In **Zhōnggúo,** restrooms are marked

with the Chinese characters 女 and 男 .

Remember also that **nán** means male
(nahn)

and **nǔ** means female.
(new)

Dùibùqǐ. Cèsùo zài nǎr?

女 stands for **nǔ**   and 男 stands for **nán.**

女

男

☐ **niǎo** *(nee-ow)* .... bird
☐ **ānchún** *(ahn-choon)* .... quail
☐ **é** *(uh)* .... goose
☐ **gēzi** *(guh-zuh)* .... pigeon
☐ **jī** *(jee)* .... chicken

鸟
niao

56

Next stop — **shūfáng**, *(shoo-fahng)* specifically **zhuōzi** *(jwoh-zuh)* or **shūzhuō** *(shoo-jwoh)* in the **shūfáng**. *(shoo-fahng)*
study   table   desk

Zhuōzi *(jwoh-zuh)* **shàng** *(shahng)* **yǒu** *(yoh)* **shénme ?** Let's identify the **dōngxi** *(dwong-ssee)* that one normally finds in the
table   on   has   what   things

shūfáng or strewn about the **fángzi.** *(fahng-zuh)*
house

---

qiānbǐ *(chee-ahn-bee)*
pencil

gāngbǐ *(gahng-bee)*
pen

zhǐ *(juhr)*
paper

xìn *(sseen)*
letter

---

gāngbǐ

---

míngxìnpiàn *(meeng-sseen-pee-ahn)*
postcard

yóupiào *(yoh-pee-ow)*
stamp

shū *(shoo)*
book

zázhì *(zah-juhr)*
magazine

---

bàozhǐ *(bow-juhr)*
newspaper

yǎnjìng *(yahn-jeeng)*
glasses

diànshì *(dee-ahn-shr)*
television

zìzhǐlǒu *(zuh-juhr-loh)*
wastepaper basket

57

Xiànzài, label these *(dwong-ssee)* **dōngxī** in your *(shoo-fahng)* **shūfáng** with your stickers. Do not forget to say
(things)   (study)

these **zì** out loud whenever **nǐ xiě** them, **nǐ** see them *(hwoh-shr)* **huòshì nǐ** apply the stickers.
                            (write)   (or)

Xiànzài identify the **dōngxī** in the *(ssee-ah-bee-ahnr)* **xiàbiānr huàr** by filling in each blank with the *(jung-choo-eh)* **zhèngquè**
                                                      (below)   (correct)

Zhōngguó zi.

1

4

5

6

2

7

8

3

9

10

1. _____

2. _____

3. _____

4. _____

5. _____

6. *míngxìnpìan*

7. _____

8. _____

9. _____

10. _____

(juhr) *(shr)* *(dwong-ts)*
Zhèr shì another **sì gè dòngcí.**
(here) (are)   (four) (M) (verbs)

(kahn-jee-ahn)   *(swong)*   *(shwee)*   *(jow)*
kànjiàn = to see   **sòng** = to send   **shuì** = to sleep   **zhǎo** = to look for

_____   _____   *shuì*   _____.

Xiànzài fill in *(ssee-ah-bee-ahnr)* **xiàbiānr** blanks with *(jung-choo-eh)* **zhèngquè zì** of these *(dwong-ts)* **dòngcí.** Practice saying
                                (below)   (correct) (form)   (verbs)

the sentences out loud many times.

58

(kahn-jee-ahn)
kànjìan
see

Wǒ _kànjìan_ **chúang.**
(chwahng)
bed

Nǐ _____ **běi.**
(bay)
quilt

Tā _____ **nàozhōng.**
(now-jung)
alarm clock

Wǒmén _____ **xǐliǎnpén.**
(ssee-lee-ahn-puhn)
wash basin

Tāmén _____ **línyù.**
(leen-yoo)
shower

(swong)
sòng
send

Wǒ _____ **xìn.**
(sseen)
letters

Nǐ _sòng_ **míngxìnpìan.**
(meeng-sseen-pee-ahn)
postcards

Tā _____ **shū.**
(shoo)
books

Wǒmén _____ **míngxìnpìan.**
(meeng-sseen-pee-ahn)
postcards

Tāmén _____ **xìn.**
(sseen)
letters

(shwee)
shùi
sleep

Wǒ zài wòfáng _____ .
(wo-fahng)
in   bedroom

Nǐ zài fángzi _____ .
(fahng-zuh)
house

Tā zài kètīng _shùi_ .
(kuh-teeng)
living room

Wǒmén zài shūfáng _____ .
(shoo-fahng)
study

Tāmén zài chúfáng _____ .
(choo-fahng)
kitchen

(jow)
zhǎo
look for

Wǒ _____ **yóupìao.**
(yoh-pee-ow)
stamps

Nǐ _____ **zhǐ.**
(juhr)
paper

Tā _____ **yǎnjìng.**
(yahn-jeeng)
glasses

Wǒmén _zhǎo_ **gāngbǐ.**
(gahng-bee)
pen

Tāmén _____ **hùar.**
(hwar)
picture

Remember that the meaning of **Zhōngguò zì** vary depending on the tone used. Notice the differences in the meanings below, review the chart on page 2 and then practice using tones by saying each **zì** out loud.

(tsahn)		*(joo)*		*(tee)*	
cān = to join		**jū** = monkey		**tī** = ladder	
cán = to destroy		**jú** = department		**tí** = to lift	
cǎn = miserable		**jǔ** = to chew		**tǐ** = body	
càn = beautiful		**jù** = large		**tì** = cautious	

☐ **nèiyī** *(nay-yee)* . . . . undershirt   _____
☐ **shùiyī** *(shwee-yee)* . . . . pajamas   衣 _____
☐ **shàngyī** *(shahng-yee)* . . . . jacket   _____
☐ **yòuyǒngyī** *(yoh-yong-yee)* . . . . swimsuit   *yi* _____
☐ **yǔyī** *(yoo-yee)* . . . . raincoat   _____

Step 15

(yoh-jee-ahn)
Yóujìan
mail

Xìanzài nǐ know how to count, how to ask **wèntí,** how to use **dòngcí** *(dwong-ts)* with the "plug-in"
                                                                              verbs

formula, how to make statements and how to describe something, be it the location of

yí gè lüguǎn *(lew-gwahn)* **hùoshì yí gè fángzide** *(fahng-zuh-duh)* **yánsè** *(yahn-suh)*. **Xìanzài** let's take the basics that **nǐ**
one (M) hotel   or   house's   color

xúexíde *(ssee-yoo-eh-ssee-duh)* and expand them in special areas that will be most helpful in your travels. What
have learned

does everyone do on a holiday? Send **míngxìnpian,** *(meeng-sseen-pee-ahn)* of course. Let's learn exactly how
                                    postcards

Zhōngguó yóujú *(yoh-joo)* works.
            post office

(sseen)
xìn . . .
letters
(dow) *(may-gwoh)*
dào Měiguó
to   America
(dow) *(ssee-bahn-yah)*
dào Xībǎnyá
to   Spain
(yeeng-gwoh)
dào Yīngguó
England
(yee-dah-lee)
dào Yìdàlì
Italy

(lew)
Lù shì Zhōngguó yóutǒngde *(yoh-twong-duh)* **yánsè** *(yahn-suh)*.
green   mailbox's   color

Zhèr shì the basic **yóuzhěng zì** *(yoh-jung)*. Be sure to practice them out loud and, **zài xiàbīanrde** *(ssee-ah-bee-ahnr-duh)*
                    postal   in   below

hùar, xǐe *(ssee-eh)* these **zì**.
       write

(sseen)
xìn
letter

(meeng-sseen-pee-ahn)
míngxìnpian
postcard

(yoh-pee-ow)
yóupiao
stamp

(dee-ahn-bow)
dìanbào
telegram

xìn _____ _____ _____ _____

☐ **xíe** *(ssee-eh)*	shoes		_____
☐ **bùxíe** *(boo-ssee-eh)*	cotton shoes	鞋	_____
☐ **píxíe** *(pee-ssee-eh)*	leather shoes	*xie*	_____
☐ **qíuxíe** *(chee-yoo-ssee-eh)*	sport shoes		_____
☐ **tǔoxíe** *(twoh-ssee-eh)*	slippers		_____

60

(bow-gwoh)
bāogǔo
parcel

(yoh-twong)
yóutǒng
mailbox

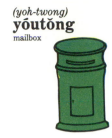

(hahng-kwong-sseen)
hángkōngxìn
air mail

HANGKONGXIN
AIR MAIL

(gwee-ti)
gùitái
counter

(dee-ahn-hwah) *(teeng)*
dìanhùa **tíng**
telephone   booth

(dee-ahn-hwah)
dìanhùa
telephone

dìanhùa

(yoh-joo)
yóujú
post office

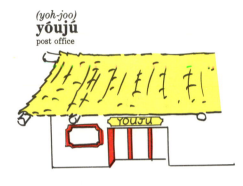

Zài Zhōnggúo, yóujú *(yoh-joo)* has everything. **Nǐ sòng xìn,** *(swong)(sseen)* **míngxìnpìan** *(meeng-sseen-pee-ahn)* and **dǎ** *(dah)* **dìanbào.** *(dee-ahn-bow)*
in   post office   send letters postcards   make telegrams

Nǐ also **mǎi** *(my)* **yóupìao** *(yoh-pee-ow)* in the **yóujú.** *(yoh-joo)*
          buy   stamps   post office

If **nǐ xǔyào** *(ssee-oo-yow)* to call home to **Měigúo,** this can be done at **yóujú** *(yoh-joo)* and is called **chángtú** *(chahng-too)*
          need   post office   long-distance

dìanhùa. *(dee-ahn-hwah)* Okay. First step — **nǐ qù** *(chee-oo)* **yóujú.** *(yoh-joo)*
telephone call   go   post office

The following **shì** *(shr)* **yí gè** *(M)* **hǎo** *(how)* sample **dùihùa.** *(dwee-hwah)* **Xìanzài** familiarize yourself with these **zì.**
              is   good   conversation

Don't wait until your holiday.

Dùibùqǐ. Wǒ zài
nǎr mǎi yóupìao?

Zài qī hào
number
gùitái.

☐ **qín** *(cheen)* . . . . musical instrument
☐ **fēngqín** *(fung-cheen)* . . . . organ
☐ **kǒuqín** *(koh-cheen)* . . . . harmonica   琴
☐ **mùqín** *(moo-cheen)* . . . . xylophone   *qín*
☐ **tíqín** *(tee-cheen)* . . . . violin

Wǒ xūyào liǎng zhāng yóupiào hé liàng zhāng míngxìnpiàn.

Hángkōngxìn ma?

Míngxìnpiàn, qī máo (7); yóupiào, yī máo (1).

Dūoshao qian?

Hǎo, hángkōngxìn. Wǒ xiǎng yào liǎng zhāng Zhōngguó míngxìnpiàn. Dūoshao qian?

Yī máo (1).

Hǎo!

Zhèr shì míngxìnpiàn hé yóupiào.

Xièxie.

Next step — **nǐ** ask **wèntí** like those **xiàbianrde,** depending upon what **nǐ** want.
(ssee-ah-bee-ahnr-duh)
below

Wǒ zài nǎr mǎi yóupiào?
(zi) (nǎhr)(my) (yoh-pee-ow)
a,n where buy stamps

Wǒ zài nǎr mǎi míngxìnpiàn?
(my) (meeng-sseen-pee-ahn)
buy postcards

Nǎr yǒu gōnggòng diànhùa?
(yoh) (goong-goong) (dee-ahn-hwah)
is public telephone

Wǒ zài nǎr dǎ chángtú diànhùa?
(nǎhr)(dǎh) (chahng-too) (dee-ahn-hwah)
where make long-distance telephone call

Wǒ zài nǎr dǎ běndì diànhùa?
(dǎh) (buhn-dee)
make local telephone call

Wǒ zài nǎr dǎ diànbào?
(dǎh) (dee-ahn-bow)
make telegram

Wǒ zài nǎr sòng bāoguo?
(swong) (bow-gwoh)
send parcel

Wǒ zài nǎr dǎ diànhùa?
(dǎh)
make telephone call

Dūoshao qian?
(dwoh-show) (chee-ahn)
how much money

Nǎr yǒu yóutǒng?
(yoh) (yoh-twong)
is mailbox

Practice these sentences again and again.

Xìanzài, quiz yourself. See if **nǐ** can translate the following thoughts into **Zhōngwèn.**

The answers are at the bottom of the **xìa ye.**
(ssee-ah) (yeh)
next page

1. Where is a telephone booth? _____ *Dìanhùa tíng zài nǎr?* _____

2. Where do I make a phone call? _____

3. Where do I make a local phone call? _____

4. Where do I make a long-distance phone call? _____

5. Where is the post office? _____

6. Where do I buy stamps? _____

7. Airmail stamps? _____

8. Where do I send a package? _____

9. Where do I send/make a telegram? _____

10. Where is counter (number) eight? *hào* _____

(juhr) *(shr)* *(jee)* *(guh)* *(dwong-ts)*
Zhèr shì jǐ ge dòngcí.
here are several (M) verbs

(dah) **da** = to make (telephone call, telegram)　　*(ssee-eh)* **xie** = to write　　*(gay)* **gei** = to give　　*(gay) (chee-ahn)* **gei qian** = to give/ pay money

_____ *dǎ* _____　　　　　　　　_____　_____

(dah) **dǎ**
make

Wǒ _____ *(dee-ahn-hwah)* **yí gè dianhùa.**
one (M) telephone call

Nǐ _____ **yí gè dianbao.** *(dee-ahn-bow)*
telegram

Tā bù *(boo)* _____ *dǎ* _____ **dianhùa.** *(dee-ahn-hwah)*
not

Wǒmén _____ **hěn dǔo dìanhùa.** *(huhn)(dwoh)*
very many

Tāmén bù *(boo)* _____ **dianbao.** *(dee-ahn-bow)*
not
telegram

(gay) **gei**
give

Wǒ _____ **tā yì běn shū.** *(tah) (buhn) (shoo)*
him (M) book

Nǐ _*gěi*_ **wǒ sì zhǎng míngxìnpìan.** *(woh) (see) (jahng) (meeng-sseen-pee-ahn)*
me four postcards

Tā _____ **tāmén hěn dǔo qían.** *(tah-muhn)(huhn) (dwoh) (chee-ahn)*
them very much money

Wǒmén _____ **tā bā zhǎng yóupìao.** *(tah) (bah) (yoh-pee-ow)*
her eight (M) stamps

Tāmén _____ **nǐ shénme ?** *(nee)*
you what

(ssee-eh) **xie**
write

Wǒ _____ **yì fēng xìn.** *(fuhng) (sseen)*
(M) letter

Nǐ _____ *xǐe* _____ **wǔ gè zì.** *(woo)*
five (M)

Tā _____ **hěn dǔo zì.** *(huhn)(dwoh)*
very many

Wǒmén _____ **shénme ?**
what

Tāmén bù *(boo)* _____ **shénme ?**
not

(gay) (chee-ahn) **gei qian**
give/pay money

Wǒ _*gěi*_ **yì běn shūde** _*qían*_. *(buhn)(shoo-duh)*
(M) book's

Nǐ _____ **qianbide** _____. *(chee-ahng-bee-duh)*
pencil's

Tā _____ **gāngbide** _____. *(gahng-bee-duh)*
pen's

Wǒmén _____ **wǔ zhǎng yóupìaode** _____. *(jahng) (yoh-pee-ow-duh)*
(M) stamp's

Tāmén _____ **shénme** _____.
what

63

Step 16

(shoh-joo) *(jahng-dahn)*
Shōujù hùoshì Zhàngdān
receipt   or   bill

(zi)   *(yow)* *(gay)*   *(chee-ahn)*   *(jahng-dahn)*
Zài Zhōnggúo, nǐ yào gěi qían for **zhàngdān. Nǐ** have just finished your evening meal and **nǐ**
in   will   give/pay money   bills

(ssee-ahng) *(yow)* *(gay)* *(chee-ahn)*   *(gay)*   *(jee-ow)*   *(foo-woo-yoo-ahn)*   *(twong-juhr)*
xiǎng yào gěi qían. Nǐ zěnme gěi qían? Nǐ jiao the **fúwùyúan:**   **"Tóngzhì!"**
would like   give/pay money   how   pay   call   service person   comrade

> **Dùibùqǐ. Wǒ**
> **xiǎng yào gěi qían.**

> **Hǎo.**

(foo-woo-yoo-ahn)
The **fúwùyúan** will normally reel off what **nǐ**
service person

have eaten, while writing rapidly. Then the

(foo-woo-yoo-ahn)   *(gay)*   *(dahn-zuh)*   *(juhr)*
fúwùyúan will **gěi** you **yì zhāng dānzi** of **zhǐ**
           give   (M)   slip   paper

(jahng-dahn)
that looks like the **zhàngdān** in the **hùar,**
          bill

while saying something like

> *(yee-goong)*   *(lee-oo)* *(yoo-ahn)*   *(mow)*
> **"Yígòng lìu yúan lìu máo."**
> altogether   six

(jahng-dahn)
Then, you will take your **zhàngdān** to the counter to pay the cashier **hùoshì nǐ gěi**
                bill   *(hwoh-shr)*   *(gay)*
                                                    or   give

(chee-ahn)
fúwùyúan qían and **zhàngdān.** The **fúwùyúan** will then bring you your change.
money

Remember that, in **Zhōnggúo,** it is not customary to leave a tip.

Also do not be surprised if the **fúwùyúan** does not thank you — this is also not a custom in

Zhōnggúo.

> **Qían zài zhèr.**

> **Xìexie.**

(sseen)   *(huh)*
Sound confusing? No, just **xīn hé** different.
                          new   and

- [ ] **dòu** *(doh)* .... bean
- [ ] **dòu fǔ** *(doh) (foo)* .... bean curd
- [ ] **dòu shā** *(doh) (shah)* .... bean paste   豆
- [ ] **dòu yá** *(doh) (yah)* .... bean sprout   *dou*
- [ ] **dòu yóu** *(doh) (yoh)* .... soybean oil

Also, remember to reserve a table in advance if you are planning to dine out in **Zhōngguó**. Give yourself enough time to enjoy a cup of **chá** and to read the *(tsi-dahn)* **càidān** _{menu} thoroughly before you decide to order. If you find, toward the end of your meal that you cannot finish, the *(foo-woo-yoo-ahn)* **fúwùyúan** will wrap up your meal for you to take with you.

To familiarize yourself with the dining customs in **Zhōngguó,** watch the other *(ruhn)* **rén** _{people} in the **fàngǔar.** At first, it seems foreign (which it is!) but **nǐ** will catch on quickly and your familiarity with **Zhōngguó** customs will be appreciated. *(juhr)* **Zhèr** _{here} *(shr)* **shì** _{is} **yí gè** _(M) sample *(dwee-hwah)* **dùihùa** _{conversation} that involves paying the *(jahng-dahn)* **zhāngdān** _{bill} when leaving a **lǚgǔan.**

Zhāng sān: *(dwee-boo-chee)* **Dùibùqǐ.** _{excuse me} **Wǒ xiǎng yào** _{would like} *(cheeng)* **qǐng** _{clear} *(jahng)* **zhǎng.** _{account}

Lǚgǔan *(jeeng-lee)* jīnglǐ: _{hotel manager} *(cheeng-wuhn)* **Qǐngwèn** _{may I ask} **nǎ gè** _{which (M)} *(fahng-jee-ahn)* **fángjiān?** _{room}

Zhāng sān: **Sān bǎi shí** *(bi)* _{hundred} **hào** *(how)* _{number}

Lǚgǔan jīnglǐ: *(ssee-eh-ssee-eh)* **Xièxie.** _{thank you} *(cheeng)* **Qǐng** _{please} *(dung)* **dēng** _{wait} *(yee)* **yí** _a *(ssee-ah)* **xìa.** _{little}

Lǚgǔan jīnglǐ: **Zhèr shì nǐde** *(nee-duh)* _{your} **zhāngdān.** *(jahng-dahn)* _{bill} **Yígòng** *(yee-goong)* _{altogether} **sān bǎi èrshíwǔ yúan.** _{hundred}

Zhāng sān: *(ssee-eh-ssee-eh)* **Xièxie.** _{thank you} (**Zhāng sān** hands him **sān bǎi sānshí yúan.**)

Lǚgǔan jīnglǐ: **Zhèr shì nǐde** *(nee-duh)* _{you} **shǒujù** *(shoh-joo)* _{receipt} **hé** *(huh)* _{and} **wǔ yúan. Xièxie.** *(ssee-eh-ssee-eh)*

Simple, right? If **nǐ** **yǒu** *(yoh)* _{have} **rénhé** *(ruhn-huh)* _{any} **wèntí** *(wuhn-tee)* _{questions} with **shùzì,** *(shoo-zuh)* _{numbers} just ask someone to write out the **shùzì** so that **nǐ** can be sure you understand everything correctly.

Qǐng *(cheeng)* _{please} **xiě** *(ssee-eh)* _{write} **chū** *(choo)* _{out} **zhè** *(juh)* _{this} **shùzì. Xièxie.** *(ssee-eh-ssee-eh)*

Let's take a break from *(chee-ahn)* **qián** _{money} and, starting on the next *(yeh)* **yè,** _{page} learn some *(sseen)* **xīn zì.** _{new}

□ **mì** *(mee)* . . . . honey _____
□ **mìfēng** *(mee-fung)* . . . . honeybee _____
□ **mìjian** *(mee-jee-ahn)* . . . . candied fruit _____
□ **mì yùe** *(mee)(yoo-eh)* . . . . honeymoon 蜜 _____
□ **mìjú** *(mee-joo)* . . . . tangerine *mi* _____

(jee-ahn-kahng)
Tā jiànkǎng.
healthy

(beeng) (luh)
Tā bìng le.
sick

(nah) (how)
Nà hǎo.
that good

(nah) (boo) (how)
Nà bù hǎo.
that not good

(nah) (hwy)
Nà huài.
that bad

(shwee) (shr) (wuhn) (duh)
Shuǐ shì wēn de.
water is warm

(woo-shr) (doo)
Shuǐ shì wǔshí dù.
fifty degrees

(lung)
Shuǐ shì lěng dé.
cold

(juhr) (shr) (shr-chee) (doo)
Zhǐ shì shíqī dù.
only is seventeen degrees

DÀ *xiao*

(ssee-ow) (shung) (shwoh-hwah)
Tā xiǎo shēng shuōhùa.
small voice speak

(dah) (shung) (shwoh-hwah)
Tā dà shēng shuōhùa.
big voice speak

(hohng) (ssee-ahn) (dwahn)
Hóng xiàn dǔan.
red line short

(lahn) (ssee-ahn) (chahng)
Lán xiàn cháng.
blue line long

(juh) (guh) (new-ruhn) (gow)
Zhè gè nǚrén gǎo.
this (M) woman tall

(ssee-ow-hahr) (i)
Zhè gè xiaohár ai.
child short

(shahng)
shàng
up

(zwoh)
zuǒ
left

(yoh)
you
right

(ssee-ah)
xìa
down

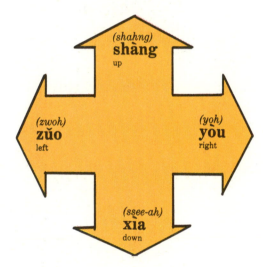

(juh) (buhn) (hohng) (hoh)
Zhè běn hóng shū hòu.
this (M) red thick

(lew) (bow)
Zhè běn lü shū báo.
(M) green thin

(yee) (jung-toh) (goong-lee)
Yì zhǒngtóu/20 gōnglǐ
one hour kilometers

(mahn)
màn
slow

(yee) (jung-toh) (goong-lee)
Yì zhǒngtóu/750 gōnglǐ
one hour kilometers

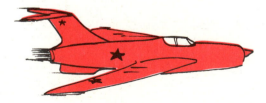

(kwy)
kuài
fast

(juh) (zwoh) (shahn) (gow) (lee-ahng)   (chee-ahn) (goong-chr) (gow)
Zhè zuò shān gāo. Liǎng qiān gōngchǐ gāo.
this (M) mountain tall   two thousand meters tall

(zwoh) (shahn) (dee) (juhr)   (goong-chr) (gow)
Zhè zuò shān dī. Zhǐ 800 gōngchǐ gāo.
(M) mountain low only   meters tall

(zoo-foo) (low)   (swee)
Zǔfù lǎo: tā 70 suì.
grandfather old   age (M)

(ssee-ow-hahr) (nee-ahn-cheeng)   (juhr) (swee)
Xiǎohár niánqīng. Tā zhǐ 10 suì.
child   young   only   age (M)

(huhn) (gwee) (yow)   (yee) (tee-ahn)
Lǚguǎn hěn guì. Yào 60 yúan yì tiān.
very   expensive costs   one   day

(goong-yoo) (pee-ahn-yee)(yow)   (tee-ahn)
Gōngyù piányì. Yào 20 yúan yì tiān.
boarding room inexpensive costs   day

(yoh)
Wǒ yǒu 1,000 yúan.
have

(yoh-chee-ahn)
Wǒ yǒuqían.
rich

(nah) (shr) (huhn) (dwoh) (chee-ahn)
Nà shì hěn duō qían.
that is   very   much   money

(juhr)(yoh)
Tā zhǐ yǒu 10 yúan.
only has

(chee-wong)
Tā qíong.
poor

(show) (chee-ahn)
Nà shì hěn shǎo qían.
little money

(juhr) (shr) (see) (guh) (sseen) (dwong-ts)
Zhèr shì sì gè xīn dòngcí.
here are four (M) new

(juhr-dow)
zhīdào = to know

(nung)
néng = to be able to/can

(yeeng-gi)
yīnggāi = to have to/ should

(kahn)
kàn = to read

zhīdào _____ _____ _____

(juhr-dow) (nung) (yeeng-gi) (kahn)
Zhīdào, néng, yīnggāi and **kàn** fall neatly into the "plug-in" formula. Whether you are
know   be able to should read

speaking about **wǒ, tā, nǐ, wǒmén** or **tāmén**, remember that verbs remain the same in

Zhōnggúo hùa.

☐ **níupái** *(nee-oo-pi)*	beefsteak	
☐ **níupí** *(nee-oo-pee)*	leather	
☐ **níupí zhǐ** *(nee-oo-pee) (juhr)*	brown paper	牛
☐ **níuròu** *(nee-oo-roh)*	beef	niu
☐ **níuwěi** *(nee-oo-way)*	ox tail	

Study the following **dòngcí** closely as you will use them a lot.

(nung)
néng
be able to/can

Wǒ _____ *(kahn)* **kàn** Zhōngwén.
read

Nǐ _*néng*_ *(shwoh)* **shūo** Zhōngwén.
speak

Tā _____ *(dwong)* **dǒng** Zhōngwén.
understand

Wǒmén _____ **dǒng** Yīngwén.

Tāmén _____ **kan** Zhōngwén.
read

(yeeng-gi)
yīnggāi
have to/should

Wǒ _____ *(shwoh)* **shūo** Zhōngwén.
speak

Nǐ _____ *(kahn)* **kàn** shū.
read

Tā _*yīnggāi*_ **shūo** Yīngwén.

Wǒmén _____ *(dwong)* **dǒng** Zhōngwén.
understand

Tāmén _____ *(kahn)* *(bow-juhr)* **kàn bàozhǐ.**
read   newspaper

(juhr-dow)
zhīdào
know

Wǒ _*zhīdào*_ *(nah)(guh)* **nà ge.**
that (M)

Nǐ _____ *(yee-dee-ahr)* **yìdiar** Zhōngwén.
a little

Tā _____ *(huhn)(dwoh)* **hěn dūo.**
very   much

Wǒmén **bù** *(boo)* _____ **hěn dūo.**
not

Tāmén **bù** _____ .

(kahn)
kàn
read

Wǒ _____ **shū.**

Nǐ _____ *(zah-juhr)* **zázhǐ.**
magazine

Tā _____ *(meeng-sseen-pee-ahn)* **míngxìnpìan.**
postcard

Wǒmén _*kàn*_ *(bee-ow-guh)* **bíaogé.**
form

Tāmén _____ *(huhn)(dwoh)* **hěn dūo.**
very   much

Nǐ *(nung)* **néng** translate these thoughts into **Zhōngwén ma?** The answers **zài xìabianr.**
can

1. I can speak Chinese. _____

2. He now should pay. _____

3. We do not know. _____

4. They can pay. _____

5. She knows very much. _____

6. I can speak a little Chinese. _____

68

(ssee-ahn)
Xiànzài draw **xian** between the **xiàbianrde** opposites. Don't forget to say them out loud.
lines   *(ssee-ah-bee-ahnr-duh)*
below

(dwong-ssee) *(nee-duh)* *(nee-duh)* *(ssee-yoo-eh-ssee-ow)(nee-duh)*
Use these **zì** every day to describe **dōngxi zài nǐde fángzi, nǐde   xúexiào,   nǐde**
things   your   your   school   your

(bahn-goong-shr)
bàngōngshì, etc.
office

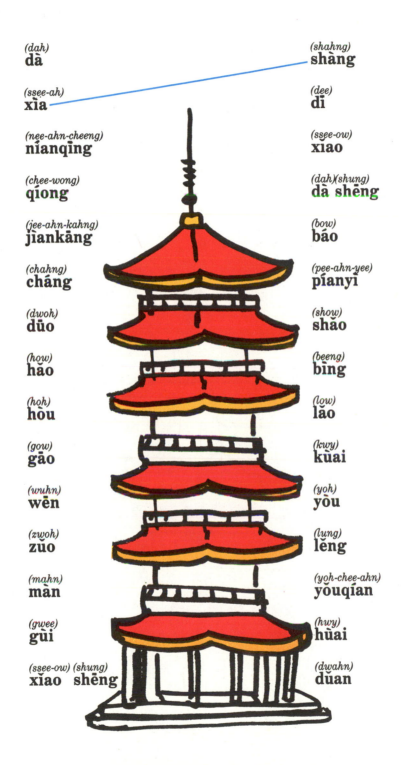

(dah) **dà**	*(shahng)* **shàng**
(ssee-ah) **xia**	*(dee)* **dǐ**
(nee-ahn-cheeng) **nianqing**	*(ssee-ow)* **xiao**
(chee-wong) **qiong**	*(dah)(shung)* **dà shěng**
(jee-ahn-kahng) **jiankāng**	*(bow)* **báo**
(chahng) **cháng**	*(pee-ahn-yee)* **pianyi**
(dwoh) **dūo**	*(show)* **shǎo**
(how) **hǎo**	*(beeng)* **bing**
(hoh) **hòu**	*(low)* **lǎo**
(gow) **gāo**	*(kwy)* **kùai**
(wuhn) **wěn**	*(yoh)* **yòu**
(zwoh) **zùo**	*(lung)* **lěng**
(mahn) **màn**	*(yoh-chee-ahn)* **yǒuqían**
(gwee) **gǔi**	*(hwy)* **hùai**
(ssee-ow) (shung) **xiao shěng**	*(dwahn)* **dǔan**

69

Step 17

(zwoh-tee-ahn) (dow)
Zúotīan dào Nánjīng!
yesterday to

(jeen-tee-ahn)
Jīntīan dào Shànghǎi!
today

(meeng-tee-ahn)
Míngtīan dào Běijīng!
tomorrow

(sseeng-chee-yee) (zi)
Xīngqīyī zài Gǔangzhōu!
Monday in

(sseeng-chee-sahn)
Xīngqīsān zài Hàngkǒu!
Wednesday

(sseeng-chee-woo)
Xīngqīwǔ zài Xīan!
Friday.

Zài Zhōnggúo, lǚxíng *(lew-sseng)* **hěn róngyì.** *(huhn)(rohng-yee)* **Zhōnggúo rén dōu hěn** *(ruhn)(doh)* **helpful. Zhōnggúo**
travel very easy people all

(huh) **hé Měigúo chàbùdūo yíyàng dà.** *(chah-boo-dwoh)(yee-yahng)(dah)* **Zài Zhōnggúo yǒu hěn dūo fāngfǎ lǚxíng:** *(yoh)(huhn)(dwoh)(fahng-fah)*
and about same size very many ways

(zwoh)(hwoh-chuh)
zùo hǔoche
by/sit train

(hwoh-shr) *(fay-jee)*
hùoshì zùo fēijī
or airplane

(goong-goong-chee-chuh))
zùo gōnggōngqìche
bus

(chwahn)
hùoshì zùo chúan
boat

(sahn-loon-chuh)
zùo sānlunchē
pedicab

(chee) (zuh-sseeng-chuh)
hùoshì qí zixíngchē.
astride bicycle

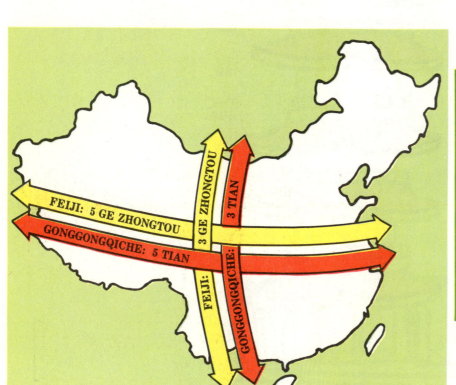

FEIJI: 5 GE ZHONGTOU

GONGGONGQICHE: 5 TIAN

3 GE ZHONGTOU

3 TIAN

FEIJI:

GONGGONGQICHE:

(zwoh-bee-ahnr)
Zǔobianr shì Zhōnggúo
left

(dee-too) (tswong) (dwong) (dow)
dìtú. Cóng dōng dào
map from east to

(fay-jee)
xī, lǚxíng zùo fēijī
airplane

(jung-toh)
wǔ gè zhōngtóu;
hours

(goong-goong-chee-chuh)
zùo gōnggòngqìchē
bus

(tee-ahn)
wǔ tīan.
days

☐ **gǔan** *(gwahn)*	place, hall	
☐ **bówùgǔan** *(bwo-woo-gwahn)*	museum	馆
☐ **chágǔan** *(chah-gwahn)*	tea house	*guan*
☐ **lǚgǔan** *(lew-gwahn)*	hotel	
☐ **lǐfàgǔan** *(lee-fah-gwahn)*	barber shop	

Zhōngguó rén bù cháng lüxíng *(ruhn)(boo)(chahng)(lew-sseeng)* themselves. Due to the amount of **wàiguó** *(wi-gwoh)* visitors in
people not often travel *foreign*

Zhōngguó, nǐ will see many "travel" **zì**. Practice saying the following **zì** many times. **Nǐ** will

see them often.

(lew-kuh)
lükè
passenger, traveler

(sseeng-lee)
xínglǐ
luggage

(ssee-ahng-zuh)
xiāngzi
trunk

(show-pee-ow) *(choo)*
shòupiào chù
ticket   office

(lew-sseeng)(shuh)
lüxíng shè
travel   agent

Xiàbianr shì some basic signs that **nǐ yě** *(yuh)* should learn to recognize quickly. **Wàng** *(wahng)* means
also

"toward" or "to" in **Zhōngguó hùa**. For example **"wàng chūkǒu"** *(wahng)(choo-koh)* means "to the exit."
exit

(roo-koh)
rùkǒu _____
entrance

(jeen)(juhr)(twong)(sseeng)
jìn zhǐ tōng xíng _____
no   trespassing

(choo-koh)
chūkǒu _chūkǒu_____
exit

(ti-peeng)(muhn)
tàipíng mén _____
emergency   gate

RUKOU

CHUKOU

TAIPING MEN

☐ **měishùguǎn** *(may-shoo-gwahn)*	art gallery		
☐ **shuǐzúguǎn** *(shwee-zoo-gwahn)*	aquarium	馆	_____
☐ **tǐyùguǎn** *(tee-yoo-gwahn)*	gymnasium	*guan*	_____
☐ **túshūguǎn** *(too-shoo-gwahn)*	library		_____
☐ **zhǎnlǎnguǎn** *(jahn-lahn-gwahn)*	exhibition hall		_____

Familiarize yourself with the following **zì**. They will help you in your **lǚxíng** *(lew-sseeng)* in **Zhōngguó**.
travel

(jee-eh)
jiē _____
street

(pee-ow)
piào _____
ticket

(ruhn-sseeng-dow)
rénxíngdào _____
sidewalk

(dah-dow)
dàdào _____ *dàdào*
boulevard

Zhèr shì sì *(see)* **gè zhòngyàode zì.**
four (M) *(jwong-yow-duh)* important

Cóng Shànghǎi dào Nánjīng *(tswong)* from *(dow)* to			
Kāi *(ki)* leave	**Huǒchē lèi** *(lay)* train type	**Dào** *(dow)* arrive	**Fùjì** *(foo-jee)* remarks
7:40	Tèkuài	8:30	✍🍴🚃📞
10:00	Kuàichē	11:10	🍴
12:15	Kuàichē	13:25	🍴🚌
14:32	Pǔtǒngchē	16:15	

(dow)
dào _____
to, arrive

(ki)
kāi _____
leave, depart

(gwoh-wi)
gúowài _____ *gúowài*
international

(gwoh-nay)
gúonèi _____
domestic

Let's learn the basic travel **dòngcí**. *(dwong-ts)* Follow the same pattern **nǐ** learned **yìqián** *(yee-chee-ahn)* with the
verbs before
"plug-in" formula.

(ki-chuh)
kāichē = to drive

(fay)
fēi = to fly

(dah)
dā = to travel/by

_____

_____

_____

(deeng)
dìng = to book, as in reserve

(jee-ahng-lwoh)
jiānglùo = to land

(dow)
dào = to arrive

_____

_____

_____

(ki)
kāi = to depart

(shahng)
shàng = to climb/ to get on

(hwahn) (chuh)
hùan (chē) = to transfer (vehicle)

_____

_____

_____

(zwoh)
zùo = to sit/by

(shahng) (chuh)
shàng (chē) = to board (vehicle)
on

(ssee-ah) (chuh)
xìa (che) = to disembark (vehicle)
down

zùo

☐ **mǐ** *(mee)* . . . . rice		
☐ **mǐfàn** *(mee-fahn)* . . . . cooked rice		
☐ **mǐfěn** *(mee-fuhn)* . . . . rice noodle	米	
☐ **mǐjǐu** *(mee-jee-oo)* . . . . rice wine	*mi*	
☐ **mǐsè** *(mee-suh)* . . . . cream-colored		

With **zhè xiē dòngcí, nǐ** are ready for any **lǚxíng** anywhere. Using the "plug-in" formula

(lew-sseeng)
travel

(dwong-ts) *(yee-chee-ahn)* *(lee-ahn-ssee-duh)*
for **dòngcí** that **nǐ yǐqián** **liànxíde,** translate the following thoughts into **Zhōngwén.**
before practiced

(ssee-ah-bee-ahnr)
The answers **zài xiàbianr.**

1. I fly to Nanjing. _____

2. I drive to Shanghai. _____

3. We land in Peking. _____

4. He sits in the airplane. _____

5. She books the trips to America. _____

6. They travel to Hangzhou. _____

7. Where is the train to Xian? _____

8. How do I fly to Japan? _____

(juhr) *(yoh)* *(sseen)*
Zhèr yòu are more **xīn zì** for your trip. As always, write out the **zì** and practice the sample
here again new

sentences out loud.

(hwoh-chuh) *(jahn)*
huǒchē zhàn
train station

(hwoh-chuh) *(zwong)* *(jahn)*
huǒchē zǒng zhàn
train main station

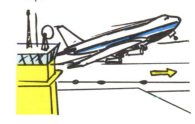

(fay-jee-chahng)
fēijīchǎng
airport

féijīchǎng

_____

(dwee-boo-chee) *(hwoh-chuh)* *(jahn)*
Dùibùqǐ. Huǒchē zhàn
excuse me train station
(zì) *(nahr)*
zài nǎr?
is where

_____

Dùibùqǐ. Huǒchē
train
(zwong) *(jahn)*
zǒng zhàn zài nǎr?
main station

_____

(fay-jee-chahng)
Dùibùqǐ. Fēijīchǎng zài nǎr?
airport

73

(dwee-hwahn) *(choo)*
dùihùan chù
money-exchange office

(shr-woo) *(jow-leeng)*
shīwù zhǎolíng
lost-and-found office

(shr-jee-ahn) *(bee-ow)*
shíjīan bǐao
time   schedule

Cóng Shanghai dào Nanjing			
(kāi) Kāi leave	**Hǔochē lèi** train type	**(dào)** Dào arrive	**Fùjì** remarks
7:40	Tèkùai	8:30	
10:00	Kùaichē	11:10	
12:15	Kùaichē	13:25	
14:32	Pútōngchē	16:15	

_____

(dwee-boo-chee) *(dwee-hwahn)* *(choo)*
Dùibùqǐ. Dùihùan chù
excuse me
(zi) *(nahr)*
zài nǎr?
is   where

(shr-woo) *(jow-leeng)*
Dùibùqǐ. Shīwù zhǎolíng
lost-and-found office

zài nǎr?

(shr-jee-ahn) *(bee-ow)*
Dùibùqǐ. Shíjīan bǐao
time schedule

zài nǎr?

(yoh-ruhn)
yǒurén _____ *yǒurén* _____
occupied

(chuh-ssee-ahng)
chēxīang _____
compartment

(zwoh-way)
zùowěi _____
seat

(juh) *(guh)* *(zwoh-way)* *(yoh-ruhn)* *(mah)*
Zhè gè zùowěi yǒurén ma? _____
this (M) seat   occupied

(chuh-ssee-ahng) *(yoh-ruhn)*
Zhè gè chēxīang yǒurén ma? _____
this (M) compartment occupied

Practice writing out the following **wèntí**. It will help you **yǐhòu**.
(yee-hoh)
later

(cheeng-wuhn) *(tsuh-swoh)*
Qǐngwèn, cèsǔo zài nǎr? _____
may I ask   lavatory

(jee-oo) *(how)* *(chuh-ssee-ahng)*
Jǐu hào chēxīang zài nǎr? _____
nine number compartment

(hoh-chuh) *(shr)*
Hòuchē shì zài nǎr? ____ *Hòuchē shì zài nǎr?* _____
waiting   room

(bah) *(how)* *(gwee-ti)*
Bá hào gùitái zài nǎr? _____
eight number counter

(kuh-yee) *(choh-yahn)* *(mah)*
Kěyǐ chōuyān ma? _____
may (I) smoke

Increase your travel **zì** by writing out the **xiàbianrde** *(ssee-ah-bee-ahnr-duh)* **zì** and practicing the sample sentences
below

out loud.

dào *(dow)* _____
to
Dào Shànghǎi de huǒchē zài nǎr?

shíjiān *(shr-jee-ahn)* _____
time
Wǒ yǒu hěn dūo shíjiān.

tiěguǐ *(tee-eh-gwee)* _____
track
Huǒchē cóng dìqī tíao tiěguǐ kāi.
seventh (M)

yùetái *(yoo-eh-ti)* _____
platform
Huǒchē dào dìbā yùetái.
eighth

Practice these **zì** every day. **Nǐ** will be surprised how often **nǐ** will use them.

Xiàbianrde nǐ néng kàn ma? *(ssee-ah-bee-ahnr-duh) (nung) (kahn)*
can read

Xiànzài nǐ zuò zài fēi dào Zhōngguó de fēiji shàng. Nǐ hùan le qian (you have, haven't
(zwoh) sit *(fay)* fly *(dow)* to *(fay-jee)* airplane *(shahng)* on *(hwahn)* have exchanged money *(chee-ahn)*

you?) **Nǐ yǒu le piao he huzhào. Nǐ dài le nide xiāngzi. Xiànzài nǐ shì yí gè lǚkè.**
(yoh) have *(pee-ow)* ticket *(huh)* and *(hoo-jow)* passport *(di)* bring *(nee-duh)* your *(ssee-ahng-zuh)* suitcase *(shr)* are (M) *(lew-kuh)* traveler

Nǐ shísì dian shiwǔ fēn zài Zhōngguó jianglǔo. Yī lù píng ān!
(shr-see) fourteen *(dee-ahn)* o'clock *(shr-woo)* fifteen *(fuhn)* minutes *(jee-ahng-lwoh)* land *(yee) (loo) (peeng) (ahn)* safe and peaceful journey

Xiànzài nǐ dàole and you **qù** to the **huǒchē zhàn** in order to get to your final destination.
(dow-luh) have arrived *(chee-oo)* go *(jahn)* train station

Zhōngguó huǒchē come in different shapes, sizes and speeds. **Zài Zhōngguó,** there are

pǔtōngchē, kùaichē hé tèbié kùaichē. Some **huǒchē yǒu cānchē.** Some **huǒchē yǒu**
(poo-twong-chuh) ordinary trains *(kwy-chuh)* fast trains *(tuh-bee-eh)* special *(kwy-chuh)* fast trains *(yoh)* have *(tsahn-chuh)* dining car

wòpù. Some **huǒchē yǒu tǎngyǐ.** All this will be indicated on the **shíjiān biǎo,** but
(wo-poo) sleeping car *(yoh)* *(tahng-yee)* reclining car *(shr-jee-ahn)* time *(bee-ow)* schedule

remember, **nǐ** should **zhīdào zěnme wèn zhè xie wèntí.** Practice your possible **wèntí**
(juhr-dow) know how *(wuhn)* to ask *(juh)* these *(wuhn-tee)* questions

by writing out the following samples.

Zhè gè huǒchē yǒu cānchē ma? *cānchē* _____
(juh) (guh) (hwoh-chuh) (yoh) (tsahn-chuh)
this (M) train has dining car

Zhè gè huǒchē yǒu wòpù ma? *(wo-poo)* _____
(M) sleeping car

Zhè gè huǒchē yǒu tǎngyǐ ma? *(tahng-yee)* _____
(M) reclining car

☐ **èryùe** *(ur-yoo-eh)* . . . . February _____
☐ **jiǔyùe** *(jee-oo-yoo-eh)* . . . . September _____
☐ **liùyùe** *(lee-oo-yoo-eh)* . . . . June 月 _____
☐ **shíyiyùe** *(shr-yee-yoo-eh)* . . . . November *yue* _____
☐ **sìyùe** *(see-yoo-eh)* . . . . April _____

What about inquiring about **jìaqían?** *(jee-ah-chee-ahn)* (prices) **Nǐ néng wèn zhè gè wèntí.** *(nung)* (can) *(wuhn)* (ask) (M)

Cóng Shànghǎi dào Běijīng dūoshǎo qían? _____
(tswong) (from) *(dow)* (to) *(dwoh-show)* (how much) *(chee-ahn)* (money)

dānchéng _____ **láihúi** _láihúi_
(dahn-chung) (one-way) *(li-hwee)* (round-trip)

Cóng Shànghǎi dào Nánjīng dūoshǎo qían? _____
(tswong) (from) *(dow)* (to)

Dānchéng hùoshì láihúi? _____
(dahn-chung) (one-way) *(hwoh-shr)* (or) *(li-hwee)* (round-trip)

Nǐ yě néng wèn: *(yeh)* (also) *(nung)* (can) *(wuhn)* (ask)

Shénme shíhòu kǎi? *(shr-hoh)* (what) (time) *(ki)* (depart)

Shénme shíhòu dào? *(dow)* (what) (time) (arrive)

Hǔochē shénme shíhòu kǎi Gǔangzhōu? _____
(hwoh-chuh) (train) (depart)

Fēijǐ shénme shíhòu kǎi Shànghǎi? _____
(fay-jee) (airplane)

Hǔochē shénme shíhòu dào Xīan? _____
(dow) (arrive)

Fēijǐ shénme shíhòu dào Běijīng? _____
(dow) (arrive)

Nǐ dàole Zhōnggúo. (have arrived) **Xìanzài nǐ zài hǔochē zhàn.** (are at) (station) **Nǐ yào qù nǎr?** *(yow)* (want) *(chee-oo)* (to go) *(nahr)* (where) **Hǎo,** *(how)* (well) tell that to the **mǎipìaodě** *(my-pee-ow-duh)* (ticket seller) at the **gùitái.** *(gwee-ti)* (counter)

Wǒ xǐang yào dào Hángzhōu qù. _____
(ssee-ahng) (would) *(yow)* (like to) *(dow)* (to) *(chee-oo)* (go)

Wǒ xǐang yào dào Sūzhōu qù. _Wǒ xǐang yào dào Sūzhōu qù._
(dow) (to) *(chee-oo)* (go)

Wǒmén xǐang yào dào Běidàihé qù.

Dào Tīanjīn de chē shénme shíhòu kǎi? _____
(dow) (to) *(chuh)* (train) (what) *(shr-hoh)* (time) *(ki)* (leave)

Dào Tīanjīn de pìao dūoshǎo qían? _____
(pee-ow) (ticket) *(dwoh-show)* (how much) *(chee-ahn)* (money)

Wǒ xǐang yào yī zhāng pìao. _____
(yee) (one) *(jahng)* (M) *(pee-ow)* (ticket)

Tǒu děng _____ **Er děng** _____
(toh) (first) *(dung)* (class) *(ur)* (second) *(dung)* (class)

Shì dānchéng hùoshì láihúi? _____
(shr) (is) *(dahn-chung)* (one-way) *(hwoh-shr)* (or) *(li-hwee)* (round-trip)

Yào hùanchē ma? _____ **Xìexie.** _____
(yow) (have) *(hwahn-chuh)* (to transfer) *(ssee-eh-ssee-eh)* (thank you)

With this practice, **nǐ zǎi** *(zi)* (are) off and running. **Zhè gè lǔxíng zì** *(juh)* (these) (M) *(lew-sseeng)* (travel) will make your holiday twice as enjoyable and at least three times as easy. Review the **xīn zì** *(sseen)* (new) by doing the

crossword puzzle on page 77. Practice drilling yourself on this Step by selecting

other locations and asking your own **wèntí** about **huǒchē,** *(wuhn-tee)* *(hwoh-chuh)* **gōnggòngqìchē** *(goong-goong-chee-chuh)* **hùoshì fēiji** *(hwoh-shr)* *(fay-jee)*

questions *trains* *buses* *or* *airplanes*

that go there. Select **xīn zì** from your **zì diǎn** *(zuh) (dee-ahn)* and practice asking **wèntí** that begin with

NÀR *(nahr)* | **SHÉNME SHÍHÒU** *(shr-hoh)* | **DŪOSHĂO QÍAN** *(dwoh-show) (chee-ahn)* | **huoshi** *(hwoh-shr)* making statements like
or

Wǒ xiǎng yào dào Shànghǎi qù. *(dow)* *(chee-oo)*
to *go*

Wǒ xiǎng yào yì zhāng pìao. *(jahng)* *(pee-ow)*
(M)) *ticket*

ACROSS

1. time schedule
4. price
6. airport
9. exit
12. passenger
14. main station
15. exchange place
16. emergency gate
18. to travel
20. recliner
21. luggage
23. one-way
24. to know
26. fast

DOWN

2. train
3. counter
5. ticket seller
7. to land
8. dining car
10. lost-and-found office
11. entrance
13. compartment
17. international
19. to disembark
22. round trip
25. sleeping car

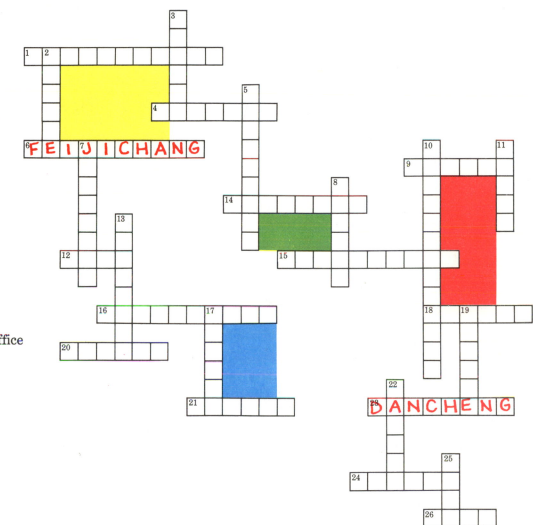

Step 18

Xiānzài nǐ zài Zhōngguó de lǚguǎn le. Nǐ è le. Nǐ xiǎng yào chīfàn. Hǎo fànguǎr
(lew-gwahn) hotel *(uh)* hungry *(chr-fahn)* to eat meal *(how)* good *(fahn-gwar)* restaurant

zài nǎr? First of all, **yǒu hěn duō chīfàn de dìfāng.** Let's learn them.
(yoh) there are *(huhn)* very *(dwoh)* many *(chr-fahn)* eating *(dee-fahng)* places

---

lǚguǎn de shítáng *(shr-tahng)* = a dining room in a hotel that serves a variety of **Zhōngguó** dishes as well as **Měiguó** dishes.

xiǎo chīdiàn *(ssee-ow) (chr-dee-ahn)* = a snack shop, usually open for breakfast, lunch and dinner.

mian guǎnr *(mee-ahn) (gwahnr)* = a noodle shop that provides a variety of noodle dishes.

jiu guǎnr *(jee-oo) (gwahnr)* = a tavern that has a limited menu but some specialties.

fànguǎr = a restaurant that serves a variety of meals, depending upon the province you are visiting.

Try all of them. Experiment. Nǐ find a **hǎo fànguǎr.** Nǐ enter and **zhǎo le yí gè**
(how) good *(jow)* look for *(M)*

zuòwèi. Nǐ **kěyǐ** share a **zhuōzi** with others, which is a common and pleasant custom in
(zwoh-way) seat *(kuh-yee)* may *(jwoh-zuh)* table

Zhōngguó. If nǐ **kànjian** a vacant **yǐzi,** just be sure to first ask
(kahn-jee-ahn) see *(yee-zuh)* chair

Duìbùqǐ. Zhèr yǒu rén ma?
(dwee-boo-chee) *(juhr)* there *(yoh)* has *(ruhn)* person *(mah)*

If nǐ **xūyào yí gè càidān,** catch the attention of the **fúwùyuán** and say
(ssee-oo-yow) need *(tsi-dahn)* *(M)* menu *(foo-woo-yoo-ahn)* service person

Duìbùqǐ. Wǒ kěyǐ yào yí gè càidān ma?
(kuh-yee) may *(yow)* have *(tsi-dahn)* *(M)* menu

☐ **shí** *(shr)* . . . . stone, rock
☐ **shígāo** *(shr-gow)* . . . . gypsum
☐ **shíkuài** *(shr-kwy)* . . . . boulder
☐ **shímò** *(shr-mwo)* . . . . graphite
☐ **shíyīng** *(shr-yeeng)* . . . . quartz

石
shi

Zài Zhōngguó, yǒu *(yoh)* **sān gè** *(sahn)* **zhòngyàode** *(jwong-yow-duh)* meals to enjoy every day, plus **xiàwǔde** *(ssee-ah-woo-duh)* snacks **hé** *(huh)*
there are   three   (M)   important   afternoon   and

wǎnshàngde *(wahn-shahng-duh)* snacks.
evening

---

zǎofàn *(zow-fahn)*	= breakfast . . . **Zài lǚguǎn, nǐ** may eat **zǎofàn** between **liù diǎn** *(dee-ahn)* o'clock and **bā diǎn.** Be sure to check the schedule before you retire for the night
wǔfàn *(woo-fahn)*	= dinner . . . . . Generally served from 11:30 to 14:30.
wǎnfàn *(wahn-fahn)*	= dinner . . . . . Generally served from 18:00 to 20:30 and sometimes later. After 21:00, only snacks will be served.

If **nǐ** look around you in a **Zhōngguó fànguǎr, nǐ** will see that **Zhōngguó rén** *(ruhn)* uses two basic
person

eating utensils: **kuàizi** *(kwy-zuh)* and **tāngchí.** *(tahng-chr)* Because all **Zhōngguó cài** *(tsi)* are cut well, knives are
chopsticks   soup spoon   dishes

generally not used. Unlike **Měiguó** customs, bowls are brought to one's mouth when

eating. Before starting your meal, you may wish the people in your party

"Nín mànman chī." *(neen)* *(mahn-manh)* *(chr)*
good   appetite

Xiànzài it may be **zǎofàn** *(zow-fahn)* time in Denver, but **nǐ zài Zhōngguó** and it is **xiàwǔ.** *(see-ah-woo)* Most
breakfast   afternoon

Zhōngguó fànguǎr post their **càidān** *(tsi-dahn)* outside. Always read it before entering so **nǐ zhīdào** *(juhr-dow)*
menu   will know

what type of meals and **jiàqian nǐ** *(jee-ah-chee-ahn)* will encounter inside. Most **fànguǎr** will also write
prices

the special meal of the day on a blackboard just inside the **mén.** *(muhn)* The meal of the day is
door

always seasonal and often consists of seafood or vegetables. In addition, all the following

main categories are on the **càidān.** *(tsi-dahn)*
menu

☐ **bǎoshí** *(bow-shr)* . . . . gem
☐ **hǎi lán bǎoshí** *(hi) (lahn) (bow-shr)* . . . . . . aquamarine   石
☐ **hóng bǎoshí** *(hohng) (bow-shr)* . . . . ruby   shi
☐ **lán bǎoshí** *(lahn) (bow-shr)* . . . . sapphire
☐ **zuànshí** *(zwahn-shr)* . . . . diamond

_____
_____
_____
_____

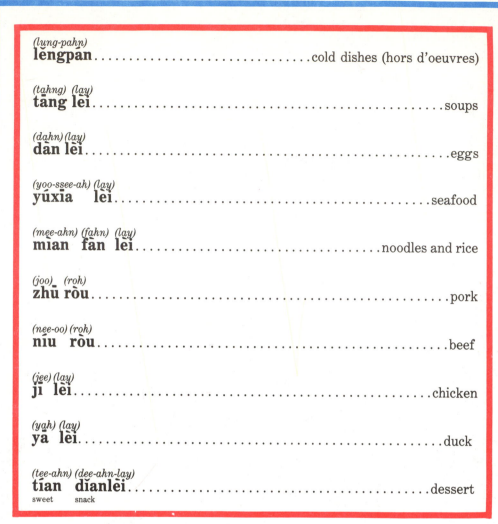

(lung-pahn)
lěngpán..cold dishes (hors d'oeuvres)

(tahng) (lay)
tāng lèi..soups

(dahn) (lay)
dàn lèi..eggs

(yoo-ssee-ah) (lay)
yúxiā lèi..seafood

(mee-ahn) (fahn) (lay)
mian fàn lèi..noodles and rice

(joo) (roh)
zhū ròu..pork

(nee-oo) (roh)
niu ròu..beef

(jee) (lay)
jī lèi..chicken

(yah) (lay)
yā lèi..duck

(tee-ahn) (dee-ahn-lay)
tián diǎnlèi..dessert
sweet snack

Most **fànguǎr** also offer **nàshǒucài**, *(ngh-shoh-tsi)* specialties which are the chef's special dishes. Because it is a custom in **Zhōngguó** to share all the dishes that one's party has ordered, make sure you know the size of the dish before you order it. The dishes will be marked in the **càidān** *(tsi-dahn)* menu as either large 大, medium 中 or small 小. At the back of this **shū**, you will find a sample **Zhōngguó càidān**. When **nǐ** are ready to leave for **Zhōngguó**, cut out the **càidān**, fold it and carry it in your pocket, wallet **huòshì** *(hwoh-shr)* or purse. **Nǐ** can **xiànzài** go into any **fànguǎr** and feel prepared!

In addition, learning the following should help you to identify what kind of meat **hùoshì** *(hwoh-shr)* or

poultry **nǐ yào jìao** *(yow) (jee-ow)* and **zěnme** it will be prepared.
want to order   how

(nee-oo-roh)
níuroù

(joo-roh)
zhǔroù

(yoo)
yú

(jee)
jī

(yah)
yā

(joo)
zhǔ = boiled

(show)
shǎo = roasted

(jah)
zhá = fried

(kow)
kǎo = baked

(jung)
zhěng = steamed

(chow)
chǎo = stir fried

Nǐ néng *(nung)* also order **qīng** *(cheeng)* **cài** *(tsi)* with your **fàn** *(fahn)*, as well as **mìan** *(mee-ahn)* or **fàn** *(fahn)*. A **tīan** *(tee-ahn)* at a **càichǎng** *(tsi-chahng)*
can   fresh   vegetables   meal   noodles   rice   day   market

will teach **nǐ** the **míngzi** *(meeng-zuh)* of different kinds of **cài hé shǔiguǒ** *(tsi) (shwee-goh)*, plus it will be a delightful
names   vegetables fruit

experience for **nǐ**. **Nǐ néng** *(nung)* always consult the menu guide at the back of this **shū** if **nǐ**
can

wàng *(wahng)* **le zhěngqǔe** *(jung-choo-eh)* **de míngzi**. **Xìanzài nǐ** have decided what **nǐ yào chī** *(chr)* and **fúwùyúan**
forget   correct   to eat

lái le. *(li)*
comes

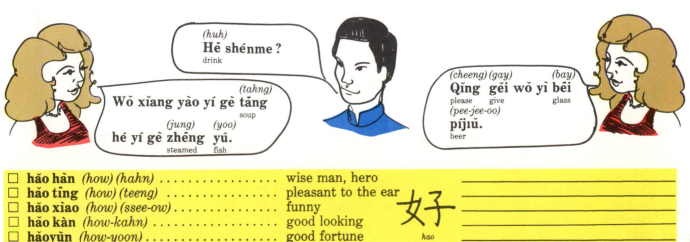

(huh)
Hē shénme ?
drink

Wǒ xǐang yào yí gè tāng *(tahng)*
soup

hé yí gè zhěng *(jung)* **yú.** *(yoo)*
steamed fish

(cheeng) (gay) *(bay)*
Qǐng gěi wǒ yì bēi
please give   glass
(pee-jee-oo)
píjiǔ.
beer

☐ **hǎo hàn** *(how) (hahn)*	wise man, hero	_____
☐ **hǎo tīng** *(how) (teeng)*	pleasant to the ear	_____
☐ **hǎo xìao** *(how) (ssee-ow)*	funny	_____
☐ **hǎo kàn** *(how-kahn)*	good looking	_____
☐ **hǎoyùn** *(how-yoon)*	good fortune	_____

好
hao

81

Don't forget that **Zhōngguó** dishes are regional and that various provinces have their own specialties. **Nǐ** won't want to miss out on the following specialties.

(tee-ahn)(jee-oo) (nee-ahng)
tián jǐu nìang
sweet rice wine

(zwong-zuh)
zòngzi
stuffed sweet rice wrapped
with bamboo leaves

(ssee-ah-roh)(hoon) (toon)
ziaròu hún tūn
shrimp and vegetables in a wrapper, boiled

(tahng-yoo-ahn)
tāngyúan
sweet rice-flour ball

(choon-joo-ahn)
chūnjǔan
pastry filled with a savory mixture of
vegetables and meat (a spring roll)

After completing your meal, call the **fúwùyúan** and **gěi qían** just as **nǐ** learned in Step 16:

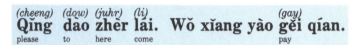

(cheeng) *(dow)* *(juhr)* *(li)* *(gay)*
Qǐng dao zhěr lái. Wǒ xǐang yào gěi qían.
please   to   here   come   pay

(tsi-dahn)
Below is a sample **cǎidǎn** to help you prepare for your trip.
menu

JĪN HǍI FǍNGǓAR

CǍIDǍN

LĚNG PÁN (cold dishes)

	Yuan
bái qie jī (cold chicken)	1.15
lǔ ya (cold duck with soy sauce)	1.20
xun yu (smoked fish)	1.50
yóu bao xīa (oil-fried shrimp)	1.75

TĀNG (soup)

xī hóng shì dàn tāng (tomato and egg soup)	1.25
yu tāng (fish soup)	1.50
dan hua tāng (egg flower soup)	1.00

ZHŪRÒU (pork)

tāng cù pai gǔ (sweet-and-sour spareribs)	2.25
gàn zha zhu pai (dry-fried fillet of pork)	2.50
qing jiao rou dìng (pork squares with pepper)	2.00
qing cai rou sī (shredded pork with vegetables)	1.95

NÍURÒU (beef)

yáng cōng níuròu (fried shredded beef with onion)	2.25
gàn bian niuroù (fried shredded beef)	2.45
chao niuroù (stir-fried beef)	2.85

HǍI WÈI (seafood)

zhá dà xīa (braised prawns)	3.25
qǐng dòu xīa rén (fried shrimp with green peas)	3.00
chao xīa pìan (stir-fried sliced prawns)	3.15
táng cù huáng yú (sweet-and-sour yellow fish)	3.25
qìng zhěng lǐ yú (steamed Mandarin fish)	3.45

FÀN (rice)

bái fàn (plain rice)	0.30
dàn chǎo fàn (fried rice with egg)	1.20
ròu sī chǎo fàn (fried rice with shredded pork)	1.45

MÌAN (noodles)

ji sī mìan (noodles with shredded chicken)	1.50
ròu sī mìan (noodles with shredded pork)	1.35
xīa rén mìan (noodles with shrimp)	1.75
chǎo mìan (fried noodles)	1.00

YǏNLÌAO (beverages)

jǐu (wine)	0.85
pijǐu (beer)	0.65
júzishǔi (orange juice)	0.55
kùang shǔi (mineral water)	0.45
kāfei (coffee)	0.45
chá (tea)	0.45

☐ **chá** *(chah)* .... tea
☐ **chábei** *(chah-bay)* .... tea cup
☐ **chádǐan** *(chah-dee-ahn)* .... light meal
☐ **chagǔan** *(chah-gwahn)* .... tea house
☐ **cháhùi** *(chah-hwee)* .... tea party

茶
cha

Zài Zhōngguó, zǎofàn *(zow-fahn)* is a very simple meal. You can eat **zǎofàn** in **nǐde lǚguǎn wūzi** *(nee-duh)* *(woo-zuh)*

or **yě kěyi** eat in the **shítáng. Zài lǚguǎn,** a western-style **zǎofàn** is **chángcháng** *(chahng-chahng)* provided *(often)*

for **lǚkè.** *(lew-kuh)* *(tourists)*

Zǎofàn ☐1 ....2.75 yúan

júzishǔi

kāfēi hùoshì chá

jīan dàn *(jee-ahn) (dahn)*
fried   eggs
tǔsī húangyóu gǔojīang *(too-see) (gwoh-jee-ahng)*
toast   butter   jam

Zǎofàn ☐2 ....2.95 yúan

júzishǔi

kāfēi hùoshì chá

jīan chángzi *(jee-ahn) (chahng-zuh)*
fried   sausage
tǔsī húangyóu gǔojīang

Zǎofàn ☐3 ....3.25 yúan

júzishǔi

hǔotǔi *(hwoh-twee)*
ham

jīan dàn

māipìan *(my-pee-ahn)*
cereal
rè qǐaokèlì *(ruh) (chee-ow-kuh-lee)*
hot   chocolate

Yǐnlìao *(yeen-lee-ow)*
beverages

kāfēi........................0.45 yuan

chá.........................0.45 yuan

júzishǔi....................0.55 yuan

☐ **chájù** *(chah-joo)* .... tea set
☐ **cháshǔi** *(chah-shwee)* .... drink (tea, etc.)
☐ **cháyè** *(chah-yeh)* .... tea leaf
☐ **hóng chá** *(hohng) (chah)* .... black tea
☐ **lǜ chá** *(lew) (chah)* .... green tea

茶
cha

83

Step 19

Zài Zhōngguó, what is different about the **dìanhùa?** *(dee-ahn-hwah)* telephone Well, **nǐ** never notice such things until **nǐ** want to use them. **Dìanhùa** allow you to **dìng** *(deeng)* make reservations in a **lǔgǔan, mǎi** my **xīpìao** *(ssee-pee-ow)* theater tickets **hé** *(huh)* and **fēijīpìao,** *(fay-jee-pee-ow)* airplane tickets contact **nǐde** *(nee-duh)* your **péngyou,** *(pung-yoh)* friends check on the hours of a **bówùgǔan,** *(bwo-woo-gwahn)* museum call a **chūchāichē,** *(choo-chi-chuh)* taxi make emergency calls and a lot of other things that **wǒmén** do **tīantīan.** *(tee-ahn-tee-ahn)* every day

Zài Zhōngguó, jīalǐ *(jee-ah-lee)* homes **bù** not **cháng** *(chahng)* often **yǒu** *(yoh)* have **dìanhùa. Zài yóujú** *(yoh-joo)* post office **yǒu** *(yoh)* there is **gōngòng** *(goong-goong)* public **dìanhùa.** Also, **zài Zhōngguó,** most streets have a **jīedào** *(jee-eh-dow)* **bàngōngshì** *(bahn-goong-shr)* street/subdistrict office in which you will **yě** *(yeh)* also find a **gōngòng dìanhùa.** Some **fēijīchǎng** *(fay-jee-chahng)* airports **hé** a few of the large shopping centers have **dìanhùa tíng.** *(teeng)* telephone booths

Zhè shì Zhōngguóde dìanhùa.

The **dìanhùa tíng** *(teeng)* booths **xìang** *(ssee-ahng)* resemble those in **Měiguó** but, as **nǐ** will see, there are some differences. This is one of those moments when **nǐ** realize,

Wǒ bú zài Měiguó.

So let's learn how to operate the **dìanhùa.**

To make a **běndì** *(buhn-dee)* local **dìanhùa,** *(dee-ahn-hwah)* telephone call **nǐ** need to first pay the **rén** *(ruhn)* person in the **jīedào** *(jee-eh-dow)* subdistrict **bàngōngshì** *(bahn-goong-shr)* office or the **rén** attending the **dìanhùa tíng.** *(teeng)* booth In a few of the **dìanhùa tíng,** you can insert **qían** in a coin box.

If **nǐ** want to make a **chángtú dìanhùa,** *(chahng-too)* you may place it through your **lǚgǔan**

service desk. **Nǐ** will be asked to fill out a form like the one **xìabīanr,** stating to whom

you are making the **dìanhùa** and to what **gúo.** *(gwoh)* country

Just to keep you on your toes, here's a fast review quiz of telephone **zì.** We've added

one—"telephone book" which translates literally as "telephone register." Can you guess

it? Draw **xìan** between the **Zhōngwén zì** and the **Yīngwén zì.**

(dee-ahn-hwah)
dìanhùa   telephone booth

(goong-goong)
gōnggòng dìanhùa   telephone book

(chahng-too)
chángtú dìanhùa   to make a telephone call

(teeng)
dìanhùa tīng   local telephone call

(boo)
dìanhùa bù   telephone

(dah)
dǎ dìanhùa   public telephone

(buhn-dee)
běndì dìanhùa   long-distance telephone call

85

So **xìanzài nǐ zhīdào** how **dǎ** *(dah)* **dìanhùa** *(dee-ahn-hwah)*. But what do **nǐ shūo** *(shwoh)* when **nǐ** finally get through

to your party? The **rén** who answers the **dìanhùa** will usually say **"Wèi"** *(way)* when **tā** picks

up the **tīngtŏng** *(teeng-twong)*. **Nǐ** should identify yourself by giving your **míngzi** and then by asking for

the **rén** you wish to speak with: **Wǒ kĕyǐ** *(kuh-yee)(guhn)* **gēn Mǎlì shūohùa** *(shwoh-hwah)* **ma?**
may   with   speak

Dìanhùa customs are not always the same! If **nǐ** are told **"Yǒu rén shūohùa,"** meaning

"There are people speaking," don't be surprised—it simply means the line is busy.

And although it means "See you again," **Zhōnggúo rén** usually say **"Zài jìan"** *(zi) (jee-ahn)*

when ending a **dìanhùade** *(dee-ahn-hwah-duh)* **dùihùa.** *(dwee-hwah)*
telephone   conversation

Xìanzài zhèr *(juhr)* **shì** *(shr)* some sample **dìanhùade dùihùa** *(dwee-hwah)*. Write them in the blanks **xìabìanr.** *(ssee-ah-bee-ahnr)*
here   are   conversations   below

Nǐ shì *(shr)* **huochē** *(hwoh-chuh)* **zhàn** *(jahn)* **ma?** _____
are   train   station

Nǐ shì bówùgǔan *(bwo-woo-gwahn)* **ma?** _*Nǐ shì bówùgǔan ma?*_
museum

Nǐ shì Jīn Hǎi Fàngǔar *(jeen) (hi)* **ma?** _____
golden sea

Nǐ shì Bĕijīng Lǚgǔan ma? _____

Nǐ shì yóujú *(yoh-joo)* **ma?** _____
post office

Nǎr *(nahr)* **yǒu** *(yoh)* **gōnggòng** *(goong-goong)* **dìanhùa?** _____
where is public

Nǎr yǒu dìanhùa bù? *(boo)* _____
book

Wǒde *(woh-duh)* **dìanhùa shì 765-8974.** _____
my

Nǐde *(nee-duh)* **dìanhùa dūoshǎo** *(how)* **hǎo?** _____
your   number

86 **Zhèr shì** another possible **dùihùa.** Listen to the **zì** and how they are used.

Christina: *(way)* **Wèi. Wǒ shì Christina. Lǐ sì tóngzhì zài ma? Wǒ kěyǐ gēn tā** *(kuh-yee)(guhn)*
hello   comrade   in   may   with

(shwoh-hwah) **shuōhùa ma?**
speak

Lǐ zǐ: **Yǒu rén shūohùa.**
the line is busy

Christina: **Wǒ zhǐ hùi shūo** *(juhr)* **yìdiǎr Zhōngwén.** *(yee-dee-ahr)* **Qǐng nǐ màn yìdiǎr shūo.** *(cheeng)(mahn)* **Hǎo ma?** *(how)*
only   a little   please   slowly   okay

Lǐ zǐ: *(dwee-boo-chee)* **Dùibùqǐ. Yǒu rén shūohùa.**
excuse me

Christina: *(ssee-eh-ssee-eh) (zì) (jee-ahn)* **Xièxie. Zài jìan.**
thanks

Here is another possible *(dwee-hwah)* **dùihùa.**
conversation

Thomas: **Wǒ xiang yào gei** *(gay)* **Zhāng sān yīshēng dǎ dìanhùa.** *(yee-shung)* **Qǐng nǐ gàosu** *(gow-soo)*
give   doctor   tell

(woh) (tah-duh) **wǒ tāde dìanhùa dūoshao.** *(dwoh-show)*
me   his   number

Dìanhùa fúwùyuán: **Tāde dìanhùa shì 827-3624.**

Thomas: **Dùibùqǐ. Qǐng nǐ zài shūo.**
say again

Dìanhùa fúwùyuán: **Tāde dìanhùa shì 827-3624.**

Thomas: **Xièxie. Zài jìan.**

Xìanzài nǐ are ready to use any **dìanhùa** in **Zhōnggúo.** Just take it **màn** *(mahn)* and speak clearly.
slowly

Don't forget **nǐ néng wèn** *(nung) (wuhn)* . . .
can   ask

Běndì dìanhùa dūoshǎo qían? *(buhn-dee) (dwoh-show) (chee-ahn)*   *Běndì dìanhùa dūoshǎo qían?*
local   telephone call   how much   money

Dǎ dìanhùa dào Běijīng dūoshǎo qían? *(dah) (dow)* _____
make   to

Dǎ chángtú dìanhùa dào Měigúo dūoshǎo qían? *(chahng-too)* _____
long-distance

Dǎ chángtú dìanhùa dào Rìběn dūoshǎo qían? *(ree-buhn)* _____
Japan

Don't forget that **nǐ xūyào** *(ssee-oo-yow)* change for the **dìanhùa!**
need

87

Step 20

(chuh)
Chē
vehicles

Zài Zhōngguó, **dìxiàtiedàochē** *(dee-ssee-ah-tee-eh-dow-chuh)* means "underground road vehicle" or subway. There

is one **dìxiàtiedàochē** *(dee-ssee-ah-tee-eh-dow-chuh)* in **Běijīng** *(bay-jeeng)* Peking but it is **bú tài cháng** *(boo) (ti) (chahng)* not too long. Most **Zhōngguó rén** travel

by **dianchē** *(dee-ahn-chuh)* trolley **huòshì gōnggòngqìchē** *(goong-goong-chee-chuh)* bus. Zài Zhōngguó, **gōnggòngqìchē** are **chángcháng** *(chahng-chahng)* often very

crowded. But **Zhōngguó rén** are very courteous to foreigners and it is not unusual

for a **lükè** to be offered a seat by a **Zhōngguó rén**. Let's learn how to take the

gōnggòngqìchē *(goong-goong-chee-chuh)*, **dìxiàtiedàochē** *(dee-ssee-ah-tee-eh-dow-chuh)* **huòshì dianchē** *(dee-ahn-chuh)*. Practice the following **zì** by saying them

aloud and by writing them in the blanks **xiàbianr**.

(dee-ssee-ah-tee-eh-dow-chuh)
dìxiàtiedàochē

(dee-ahn-chuh)
dianchē

(goong-goong-chee-chuh)
gōnggòngqìchē

dìanchē

_____ _____ _____

(chuh) (jahn)
chē zhan = (vehicle) stop _____

(loo)
lü = route _____

(see-jee)
sījī = driver _____

(chah-pee-ow-yoo-ahn)
chápiaoyuan = conductor _____

Let's also review the "transportation" **dòngcí** *(dwong-ts)* at this point.

(shahng) (chuh)
shàng chē = to board
on (vehicle)

(ssee-ah) (chuh)
xià chē = to disembark
down (vehicle)

_____   _____

(hwahn) (chuh)
hùan chē = to transfer
(vehicle)

(lew-sseeng)
lüxíng = to travel

lüxíng

_____

(dee-too)
Dìtú displaying the various **chē zhàn hé lù** are available at most major stops. Be sure
maps   *(chuh) (jahn)*   *(loo)*
                                 stops   routes

(chah-pee-ow-yoo-ahn)
to let the **chápìaoyúan** know where you are going, because ticket prices are based on
conductor

(goong-goong-chee-chuh)   *(dee-ahn-chuh)*
distances traveled. This applies to both **gōnggòngqìchē** and **dìanchē.** **Xìabìanr** is a
                                           bus   trolley

(dee-too)
dìtú that shows several places you may want to travel to by **gōnggòngqìchē** or **dìanchē**
map

(chah-pee-ow-yoo-ahn)
in any **Zhōnggúo** city. Practice the **zì** by repeating them aloud, so the **chápìaoyúan** will
                                                                   conductor

know exactly what you mean when you tell him where you are going.

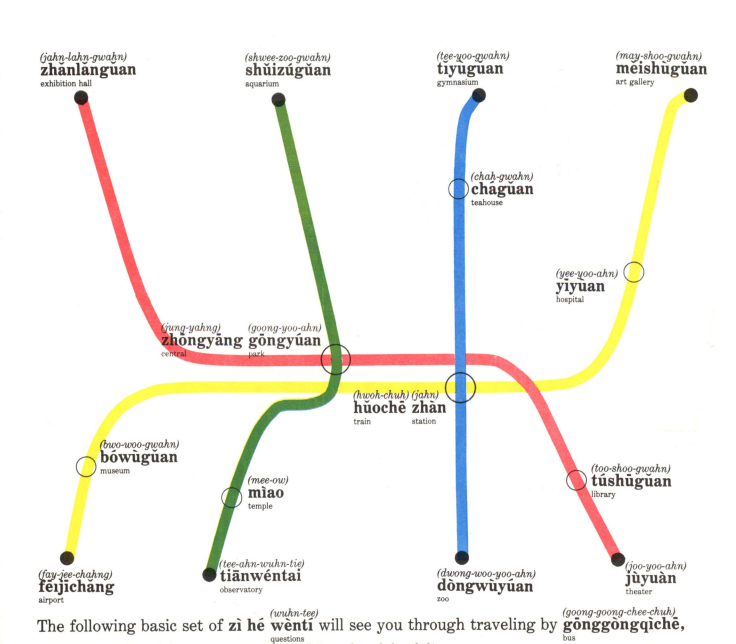

The following basic set of **zì hé wèntí** will see you through traveling by **gōnggòngqìchē,**
(wuhn-tee)   *(goong-goong-chee-chuh)*
questions   bus

(dee-ahn-chuh)   *(hwoh-chuh)*   *(dee-ssee-ah-tee-eh-dow-chuh)*
dìanchē, **hǔochē** or by **Běijīngde dìxìatīedàochē.**
trolley   train   Peking's   subway

Naturally, the first **wèntí shì "nǎr."**
(nahr)
where

(nahr) (shr) (goong-goong-chee-chuh) _(jahn)_
Nǎr shì gònggòngqìchē zhàn?
where is bus stop

(dee-ahn-chuh)(jahn)
Nǎr shì diànchē zhàn?
trolley stop

(dee-ssee-ah-tee-eh-dow-chuh) (jahn)
Nǎr shì dìxiàtiedàochē zhàn?
subway stop

Practice the following basic **wèntí** out loud and then **xiě** them in the blanks **zài yòubīanr.**
(ssee-eh) _(zi) (yoh-bee-ahnr)_
write at

(goong-goong-chee-chuh) _(jahn)_ _(zi)_ _(nahr)_
1. **Gōnggòngqìchē zhàn zài nǎr?**_____
bus stop is where
(dee-ahn-chuh)
Diànchē zhàn zài nǎr?_____
trolley
(dee-ssee-ah-tee-eh-dow-chuh)
Dìxiàtiedàochē zhàn zài nǎr?_____
subway

(shr-hoh) _(dow)_
2. **Gōnggòngqìchē shénme shíhòu dào?**_____
what time arrives

Diànchē shénme shíhòu dào?_____

Dìxiàtiedàochē shénme shíhòu dào?_____

(shr-hoh) _(ki)_
3. **Gōnggòngqìchē shénme shíhòu kāi?**_____
what time leaves

Diànchē shénme shíhòu kāi? *Diànchē shénme shíhòu kāi?*

Dìxiàtiedàochē shénme shíhòu kāi?_____

(ki) (dow) (bwo-woo-gwahn)
4. **Gōnggòngqìchē kāi dào bówùguǎn ma?**_____
goes to museum
(dwong-woo-yoo-ahn)
Diànchē kài dào dòngwùyúan ma?_____
zoo

Dìxiàtiedàochē kāi dào lǚguǎn ma?_____

(dow) _(dwoh-show) (chee-ahn)_
5. **Gōnggòngqìchē dào bówùguǎn dūoshǎo qían?**_____
to how much money

Diànchē dào dòngwùyúan dūoshǎo qían?_____

Dìxiàtiedàochē dào lǚguǎn dūoshǎo qían?_____

Xìanzài nǐ are in the swing of things, practice the following patterns aloud,

(goong-goong-chee-chuh) _(dee-ahn-chuh)_
90 substituting **gōnggòngqìche** for **diànchē** and so on.
bus trolley

1. *(my)* Zài năr **măi** gōnggòngqìchē *(pee-ow)* **pìao**? Dìanchē **pìao**? *(dee-see-ah-tee-eh-dow-chuh)* Dìxìatĭedàochē pìao?
   buy   ticket

2. *(dow)* Dào lŭgŭan, *(goong-goong-chee-chuh)* gōnggòngqìchē shénme *(shr-hoh)* shíhòu kāi? Dào bówùgŭan, *(bwo-woo-gwahn)* gōnggòngqìchē
   to   bus   what   time   leaves   museum

   shénme shíhòu kāi? Dào *(chah-gwahn-duh)* chágŭan, gōnggòngqìchē shénme shíhòu kāi?
                          tea house

3. *(chee-oo)* Qù *(chah-gwahn-duh)* chágŭande gōnggòngqìchē *(jahn)* zhàn zài năr?
   to   tea house's   stop
   (chee-oo) Qù *(tee-yoo-gwahn-duh)* tĭyùgŭande dìanchē zhàn zài năr?
   to   gymnasium's
   (may-shoo-gwahn-duh) Qù mĕishùgŭande gōnggòngqìchē zhàn zài năr?
   art gallery
   (jahn-lahn-gwahn) Qù zhănlăngŭan dìanchē zhàn zài năr?
   exhibition hall's
   (yee-yoo-ahn-duh) Qù yīyŭande dìxìatĭedàochē zhàn zài năr?
   hospital's
   (dwong-woo-yoo-ahn-duh) Qù dòngwùyúande gōnggòngqìchē zhàn zài năr?
   zoo's
   (jung-yahng) Qù zhōngyāng *(goong-yoo-ahn-duh)* gōngyúande dìanchē zhàn zài năr?
   central   park's
   (bwo-woo-gwahn-duh) Qù bówùgŭande dìxìatĭedàochē zhàn zài năr?
   museum's

(kahn) Nĭ **kàn** the following *(dee-ahng-ssee-duh)(dwee-hwah)* **dĭanxíngde dùihùa** and *(ssee-eh)* **xĭe** the **dùihùa** in the blanks **zài** *(yoh-bee-ahnr)* **yòubīanr**.
read   typical   conversations   write   right

(loo) (chee-ow) (dwong-woo-yoo-ahn) Nă yí **lù** qù dòngwùyúan?_____
which (M) route to zoo
(chee) Qí **lù**._____
seven
Qí lù chē shénme *(shr-hoh)* *(dow)* shíhòu dào?_____
              what   time   arrives
(shr) (fuhn) Shí fēn zhōng._____
ten minutes
(yow) (boo) *(hwahn-chuh)* Yào bú yào hùanchē? *yào bú yào hùanchē?*_____
must   transfer
(yow) *(jung-yahng)* *(goong-yoo-ahn-duh)* Yào, zài zhōngyāng gōngyúande zhàn hùanchē._____
yes   central   park's
(tswong) (juhr) (dow) *(yow) (dwoh-show)* Cóng zhĕr dào dòngwùyúan yào dūoshăo shíhòu?_____
from here to   takes how much
(yow) (ur-shr) Yào èrshí fēn zhōng._____
takes twenty
(pee-ow) Pìao dūoshăo qían?_____
ticket
Yì máo qían._____   91

Nǐ néng translate the following thoughts into **Zhōngwén ma?** The answers **zài xiàbianr.**

1. Where is the bus stop?_____

2. What costs a ticket to Peking?_____

3. What time does route seven arrive?_____

4. Where buy I a ticket?_____

5. Where is the streetcar stop?_____

6. I would like to get out._____

7. Must I transfer?_____

8. Where must I transfer? *zài nǎr hùanchē?*_____

Zhèr shì another **sān gè** (dwong-ts) **dòngcí.**
(M)   verbs

(ssee) **xǐ** = to wash   (dee-oo) **diū** = to lose   (yow) **yào** = to take (time)

_____   _____   _____

Nǐ zhīdào (juhr-dow) the basic "plug-in" formula, so translate the following thoughts with these
know

(sseen) **xīn dòngcí.** The answers (yeh) **yě zài xiàbianr.**
new   also

1. I wash the jacket._____

2. You lose the book._____ *Nǐ diūle shū.*_____

3. It takes 20 minutes to the museum._____

4. It takes three hours with a car._____

ANSWERS

1. **Gōnggòngqìchē zhàn zài nǎr?**
2. **Dào Běijīng duōshǎo qián?**
3. **Qǐ lù chē shénme shíhòu dào?**
4. **Wǒ zài nǎr mǎi piào?**
5. **Diànchē zhàn zài nǎr?**
6. **Wǒ xiǎng yào xiàchē?**
7. **Yào bù yào huànchē?**
8. **Zài nǎr huànchē?**

1. **Wǒ xǐ zhè shàngyī.**
2. **Nǐ diūle shū.**
3. **Yào èrshí fēn zhōng dào bówùguǎn.**
4. **Yào zuò sān gè zhōngtóu qìchē?**

(my) (my)
Mǎi hé Mài
sell buy

Zài wàiguó, (*wi-gwoh*)
foreign country
shopping is very **yòuyìsi.** (*yoh-yee-see*)
interesting
The simple everyday task of buying **yì píng níunǎi** (*peeng*) (*nee-oo-ni*)
bottle milk

hùoshì yí gè pìngguǒ (*peeng-gwoh*)
(M) apple
becomes a challenge that **nǐ xìanzài** should be able to meet quickly

and easily. Of course, **nǐ** will purchase **jìnianpǐn,** (*jee-nee-ahn-peen*)
souvenirs
yóupìao hé mǐngxìnpìan, (*yoh-pee-ow*) (*meeng-sseen-pee-ahn*)
stamps postcards
but do not

forget those many other **dōngxi** (*dwong-ssee*)
things
ranging from shoelaces to aspirin that **nǐ** might need

unexpectedly. **Nǐ zhīdào** (*juhr-dow*)
know
the difference between **yí gè shūdìan hé yí gè yàofáng ma?** (*shoo-dee-ahn*) (*yow-fahng*)
(M) bookstore (M) pharmacy

Let's learn about the different **shāngdìan** (*shahng-dee-ahn*)
stores
in **Zhōngguó. Xìabīanr shì yí gè dìtú** (*dee-too*)
(M) map
of a

typical **Zhōngguó chéngshì.** (*chung-shr*)
city

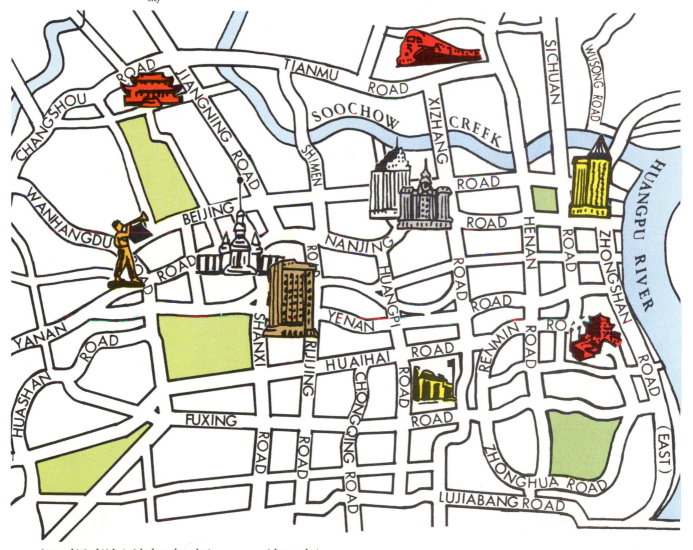

Zài xìa (*ssee-ah*)
next
yè shì (*yeh*)(*shr*)
pages are
shāngdìan (*shahng-dee-ahn*)
stores
in this **chéngshì.** (*chung-shr*)
city
Be sure to fill in each blank below the

hùar with the **shāngdìande míngzi.** (*shahng-dee-ahn-duh*)
shop's

(mee-ahn-bow) (dee-ahn)
mìanbāo dìan
bakery
(my) (mee-ahn-bow)
Năr măi mìanbāo.
buy bread

(roh) (dee-ahn)
ròu dìan
butcher's
(my) (roh)
Năr măi rōu.
buy meat

(ssee) (yee) (dee-ahn)
xĭ yī dìan
laundry
(ssee) (yee-foo)
Năr xĭ yīfú.
wash clothes

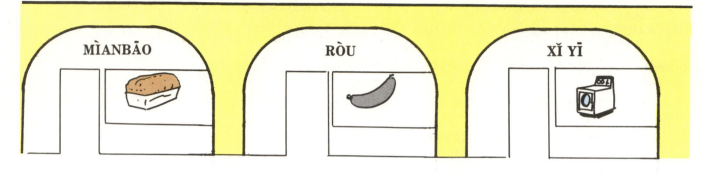

MÌANBĀO

RÒU

XĬ YĪ

(kah-fay) (dee-ahn)
kāfēi dìan
coffee shop
(huh) (kah-fay)
Năr hē kāfēi.
drink coffee

(jah-hwoh) (dee-ahn)
záhùo dìan
drug store
(fay-zow)
Năr mai feizào.
soap

(yow) (dee-ahn)
yào dìan
pharmacy
(ah-see-pee-leen)
Năr măi āsipílín.
aspirin

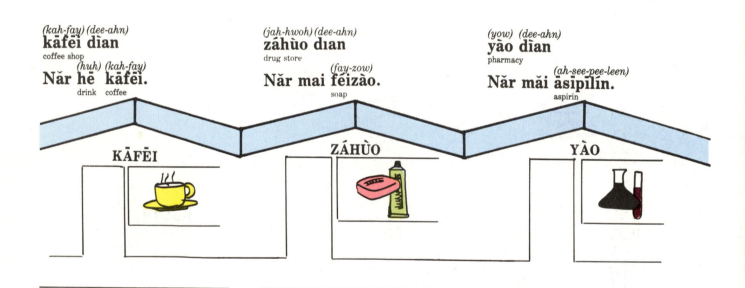

KĀFĒI

ZÁHÙO

YÀO

(hwar) (dee-ahn)
hūar dìan
flower shop
(hwar)
Năr măi hūar.
flowers

(yahn) (dee-ahn)
yān dìan
tobacco store
(yahn)
Năr măi yān.
tobacco

(tahng-gwoh) (dee-ahn)
tánggŭo dìan
candy
(tahng-gwoh)
Năr măi tánggŭo.
candy

HŪAR

YĀN

TÁNGGŬO

(nee-oo-ni) (dee-ahn)
níunǎi dìan
dairy

Nǎr mǎi níunǎi. *(nee-oo-ni)*
milk

(jow-ssee-ahng) (chee-tsi) (dee-ahn)
zhàoxìang qìcái dìan
camera store

Nǎr mǎi dìpìan. *(dee-pee-ahn)*
film

(tsi) (dee-ahn)
cǎi dìan
vegetable store

Nǎr mǎi qīngcài. *(cheeng-tsi)*
fresh vegetables

NÍUNǍI   ZHÀOXÌANG QÌCAÍ   CÀI

(teeng-chuh) (chahng)
tíngchě chǎng
parking lot

Nǎr tíng chē. *(teeng) (chuh)*
park   cars

(lee-fah) (dee-ahn)
lǐfǎ dìan
hairdresser's

Nǎr lǐ fà. *(lee) (fah)*
cut   hair

(tsi-fung) (dee-ahn)
cáiféng dìan
tailor's

Nǎr zùo yìfú. *(zwoh) (yee-foo)*
make   clothes

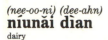

TÍNGCHĚ

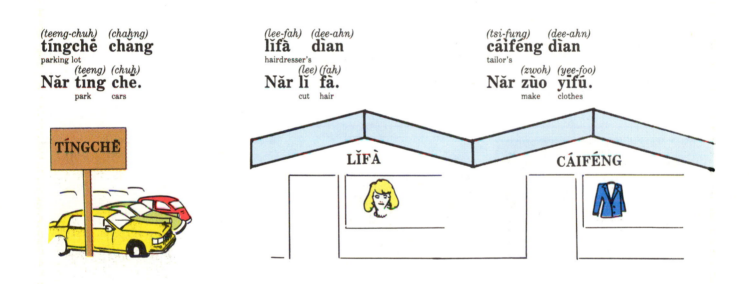

LǏFÀ   CÁIFÉNG

(yoh-joo)
yóujú
post office

Nǎr mǎi yóupìao. *(yoh-pee-ow)*
stamps

(goo-dwong) (dee-ahn)
gǔdōng dìan
antique store

Nǎr mǎi gǔdōng. *(goo-dwong)*
antiques

(yeen-hahng)
yínháng

Nǎr hùan qían. *(hwahn) (chee-ahn)*
exchange   money

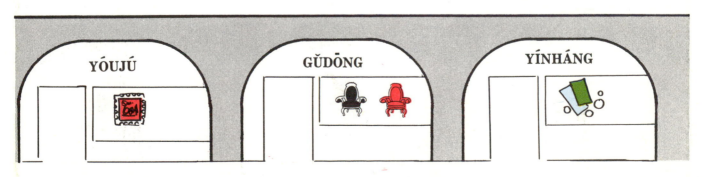

YÓUJÚ   GǓDŌNG   YÍNHÁNG

(shr-peen) *(dee-ahn)*
shìpǐn dìan
grocery store

Nǎr mǎi ròu, shǔiguǒ
(roh) *(shwee-gwoh)*
meat   fruit

huòshì níunǎi.
(nee-oo-ni)
milk

(ur-huhn) *(poo)*
èrhǔn pù
delicatessen

Nǎr mǎi shú shí.
(shoo) *(shr)*
cold   cuts

(shwee-gwoh) *(dee-ahn)*
shǔiguǒ dìan
fruit store

Nǎr mǎi shǔiguǒ.
(shwee-gwoh)
fruit

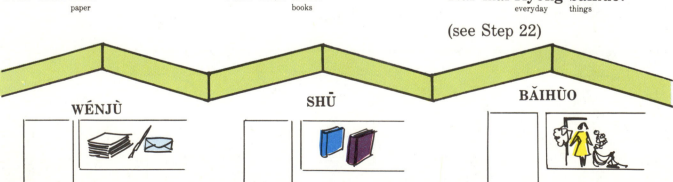

SHÍPǏN   ÈRHǓN PÙ   SHǓIGUǑ

(dee-ahn-yeeng-yoo-ahn)
dìanyǐngyùan
movie theater

Nǎr kàn dìanyǐng.
(kahn) *(dee-ahn-yeeng)*
see   movie

(shoo-bow) *(tahn)*
shūbào tān
book stand

Nǎr mǎi bàozhǐ, zázhì,
(bow-juhr) *(jah-juhr)*
newspapers   magazines

hé shǔ.
(shoo)
books

(gahn-ssee) *(dee-ahn)*
gānxǐ dìan
dry cleaner's

Nǎr gānxǐ yìfú.
(gahn-ssee) *(yee-foo)*
dry clean   clothes

DÌANYǏNGYÙAN

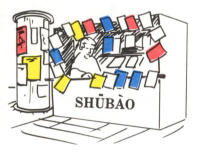

SHŪBÀO

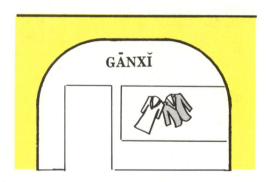

GĀNXǏ

(wuhn-joo) *(dee-ahn)*
wénjù dìan
stationery store

Nǎr mǎi zhǐ.
(juhr)
paper

(shoo) *(dee-ahn)*
shū dìan
bookstore

Nǎr mǎi shǔ.
(shoo)
books

(bi-hwoh) *(dee-ahn)*
bǎihùo dìan
department store

Nǎr mǎi rìyòng bǎihùo.
(ree-yong) *(bi-hwoh)*
everyday   things

(see Step 22)

WÉNJÙ   SHŪ   BǍIHÙO

(tsi-chahng
cáichǎng
market
(my) (cheeng) (tsi)
Nǎr mǎi qīng cài
buy fresh vegetables
(shwee-gwoh)
hé shuǐguǒ.
fruit

(jee-nee-ahn-peen) (dee-ahn)
jìnìanpǐn dìan
souvenir store
(jee-nee-ahn-peen)
Nǎr mǎi jìnìapǐn.
souvenirs

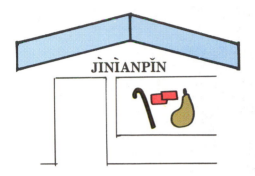

(jee-ah-yoh) (jahn)
jīayóu zhǎn
gasoline station
(chee-yoh)
Nǎr mǎi qiyou.
gasoline

(lew-sseeng) (shuh)
lǚxíng shè
travel agency
(fay-jee-pee-ow)
Nǎr mǎi fēijīpìao.
airplane ticket

(jung-bee-ow) (dee-ahn)
zhōngbǐao dìan
watchmaker's
(jung)
Nǎr mǎi zhōng
clocks
(bee-ow)
hé bǐao.
watches

(yoo) (dee-ahn)
yú dìan
fish store
(yoo)
Nǎr mǎi yú.
fish

(shahng-dee-ahn) *(shun-muh) (shr-hoh) (ki)* *(chee) (tee-ahn)*
Zài Zhōngguó, shāngdìan shénme shíhòu kāi? Normally, **shāngdìan** are open **qī tian** per
shops what time open seven days
(sseeng-chee) (shahng-woo) (jee-oo) (dee-ahn)(dow) (ssee-ah-woo) (lee-oo) (dee-ahn) (shr-jee-ahn-bee-ow)
xīngqī from **shàngwǔ jǐu dǐan dào xìawǔ lǐu dǐan.** Of course, **shíjīanbīao** vary from
week morning nine o'clock to afternoon six o'clock hours

shāngdìan to **shāngdìan.** Usually, **shāngdìan** remain open during the lunch hour and, on

(sseeng-chee-tee-ahn)
xīngqītian, most **shāngdìan** extend their shopping hours.
Sundays

Is there anything else that makes **Zhōngguó shāngdìan** different from **Měiguó**

shāngdìan? To find out, look at the **hùar** on the following **yè.**
(yeh)
page

sì lóu

sān lóu

èr lóu

yī lóu

Contrary to European custom, where the first floor is called the ground floor, in **Zhōngguó**

(and in **Měiguó**), the first floor is exactly what it says! **Xìanzài** that **nǐ** know the

(meeng-zuh)
míngzi for **Zhōngguo shāngdìan,** let's practice shopping.
names   *(shahng-dee-ahn)*
                     stores

I.   First step — Nǎr?

(nee-oo-ni) (dee-ahn)(zi) (nahr)
Níunǎi dìan zài nǎr?
dairy   is   where

(yeen-hahng)
Yínháng zài nǎr?
bank

(dee-ahn-yeeng-yoo-ahn)
Dìanyǐngyùan zài nǎr?
movie theater

Go through the **shāngdìan** introduced in this Step and ask **"nǎr"** with each **shāngdìan**.
(shahng-dee-ahn)
stores

Another way of asking **"nǎr"** is to say

(foo-jeen) (yoh)
Fùjìn yǒu níunǎi dìan ma?
vicinity has

(foo-jeen)   (yeen-hahng)
Fùjìn yǒu yínháng ma?
vicinity   bank

Go through the **shāngdìan** again using this new **wèntí.**

II.   Next step — tell them what nǐ xūyào hùoshì xiǎng yào.
(ssee-oo-yow)   *(ssee-ahng) (yow)*
need   would   like

1) **Wǒ xūyào . . .** _____ *Wǒ xūyào*
(ssee-oo-yow)
need

2) **Nǐmén yǒu . . . ma?** _____
you   *(yoh)*
           have

98 3) **Wǒ xiǎng yào . . .** _____
(ssee-ahng) (yow)
would   like

(ssee-oo-yow) *(peeng-gwoh)*
Wǒ xūyào yí gè pínggǔo.
need (M) apple

(yoh)
Nǐmén yǒu pínggǔo ma?
you have

(ssee-ahng) (yow)
Wǒ xiǎng yào yí gè pínggǔo.
would like (M)

(peeng) (kwahng) (shwee)
Wǒ xūyaò yì píng kuàng shǔi.
bottle mineral water

(kwahng) (shwee)
Nǐmén yǒu kùang shǔi ma?
mineral water

(peeng)
Wǒ xiǎng yào yì píng kuàng shǔi.
bottle

Go through the glossary at the end of this **shū** and select **èrshí gè zì.** *(ur-shr)* Drill the above
twenty (M)

patterns with **zhè èrshí gè zì.** Don't cheat. Drill them **jīntīan.** *(jeen-tee-ahn)* **Xìanzaì,** take **èrshí**
(M) today

gè zì more from **nǐde zì diǎn** *(zuh)(dee-ahn)* and do the same. And don't just drill them **jīntīan.**
(M) dictionary

Take more **zì mīngtīan** *(meeng-tee-ahn)* and drill them also.
tomorrow

III. Next step — find out dūoshǎo qían.
(dwoh-show) *(chee-ahn)*
how much money

1) *(nah)* *(dwoh-show)*
Nà gè dūoshǎo? _____
that (M) how much

2) **Nà gè dūoshǎo qían?** *(chee-ahn)*
(M) money

(chee-ahn-bee)
Qīanbǐ dūoshǎo?
pencil
(meeng-sseen-pee-ahn)
Míngxìnpìan dūoshǎo qían?
postcard
(yoh-pee-ow)
Yóupìao dūoshǎo qían?
stamp

(peeng-gwoh)
Pínggǔo dūoshǎo?
apple
(joo-zuh)
Júzi dūoshǎo?
orange
(kwahng) (shwee)
Kùang shǔi dūoshǎo qían?
mineral water

Using these same **zì** that **nǐ** selected **shàngbīanr,** *(shahng-bee-ahnr)* **yě** *(yeh)* drill these **wèntí.**
above also

IV. If nǐ bù *(boo)* **zhīdào** *(juhr-dow)* where to find something, **nǐ wèn** *(wuhn)*
don't know ask

(my) *(ah-see-pee-leen)*
Nǎr mǎi āsīpǐlín?
buy aspirin

(ti-yahng) *(yahn-jeeng)*
Zài nǎr mǎi tàiyáng yǎnjìng?
sun glasses

Once **nǐ zhīdào** *(juhr-dow)* what **nǐ** want, **nǐ shūo,** *(shwoh)*
know say

Wǒ xiǎng yào zhè gè. *(juh) (guh)*
this (M)

Hùoshì, if **nǐ** don't want something, **nǐ shūo,**

Wǒ bù xǐhuan nà gè. *(boo) (ssee-hoo-ahn)(nah)*
not like that (M)

Xìanzaì nǐ are all set to shop for anything!

99

(bi-hwoh) **Bǎihùo** *(dee-ahn)* **Dìan**
department   store

At this point, **nǐ** should just about be ready for **nǐde Zhōnggúo lǚxíng.** **Nǐ** have gone

shopping for those last-minute odds 'n ends. Most likely, the store directory at your

local **bǎihùo dìan** *(bi-hwoh)* *(dee-ahn)* does not look like the one **xìabianrde.** *(ssee-ah-bee-ahnr-duh)* **Nǐ** already **zhīdào hěn dūo** *(juhr-dow) (huhn) (dwoh)*
department   store   below   know   very   many

zì and **nǐ** could guess at **hěn dūo** others. **Nǐ zhīdào xǐaohár shì Zhōngwén** *(ssee-ow-hahr)* for children,

so if **nǐ xūyào** *(ssee-oo-yow)* something for the **xǐaohár,** *(ssee-ow-hahr)* **nǐ** would probably look on **sān lóu.** *(loh)*
      need   floor

7. LÓU	mìanbāo shítáng shú shí yǐnlìao	jī yā càichǎng shuǐguo qīng cài	wàigúo shípǐn jǐu yě wèi ròu lèi
6. LÓU	chúang tǎnzi hé bèi sùlìao pǐn	jīajù dēng dòngfāng hùo	dìtǎn hùar
5. LÓU	yínqì dìanqì pǐn bōlí	jīatíng yòngpǐn shìhào yòngpǐn chúfáng jīajù	yàochí táoqì cíqì
4. LÓU	shū dìanshì értóng jīajù yīngér yòngpǐn	wánjù yùeqì shòuyīnjī wénjù chàng pìan	yān cháshì zázhì bàozhǐ
3. LÓU	záhùo nǚrén yīfú	nánrén yīfú nǚrén màozi	shìwù zhǎolǐng gùkè fúwù
2. LÓU	qìchē yòngpǐn nǚrén nèiyīkù shǒujùar	yùshì yòngpǐn xíe gōngjù	chúang dǎn yùndòng yòngpǐn
1. LÓU	zhàoxìang yòngpǐn nánrén màozi sǎn zhūbǎo	shǒutòur pízhì pǐn wàzi zhōngbìao	nánrén yòngpǐn xīangshuǐ tángǔo

Let's start a checklist for **nǐde lǚxíng.** Besides **yīfú,** *(yee-foo)* **nǐ hǎi xūyào shénme?** *(hi)*
                                                     clothing   still   need   what

For your trip, **nǐ yīnggāi** *(yeeng-gi)* **ná** *(nah)* **shénme?**
               should   take

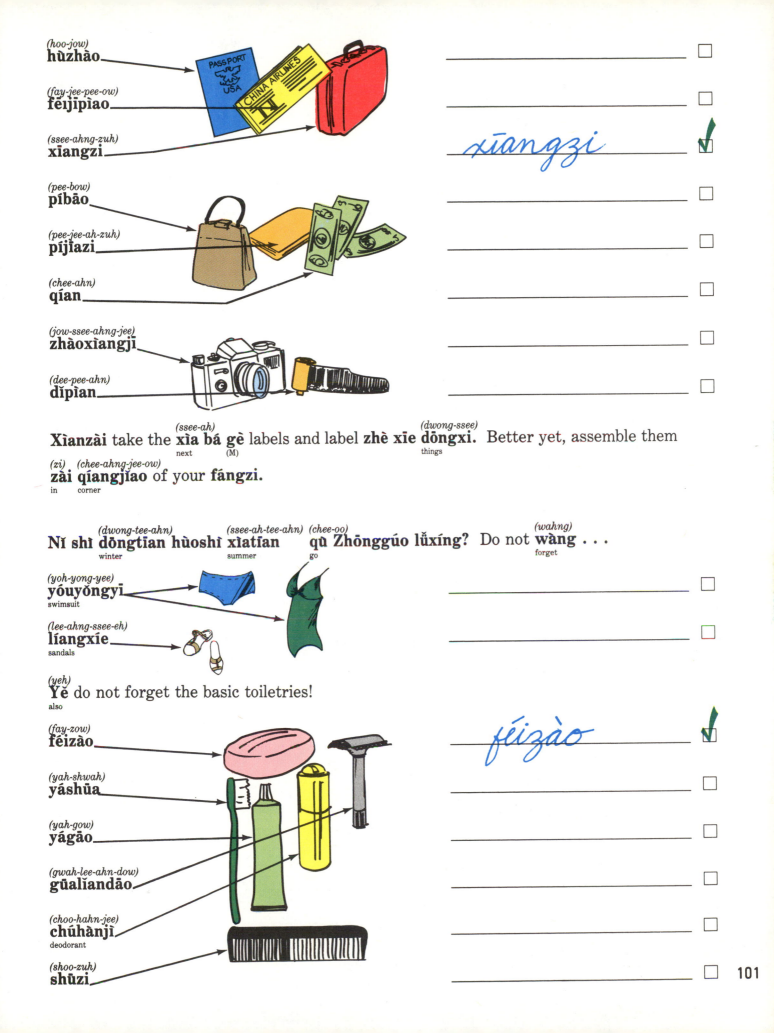

(hoo-jow)
hùzhào

(fay-jee-pee-ow)
fēijīpiào

(ssee-ahng-zuh)
xīangzi

xīangzi ✓

(pee-bow)
píbāo

(pee-jee-ah-zuh)
píjiazi

(chee-ahn)
qían

(jow-ssee-ahng-jee)
zhàoxīangjī

(dee-pee-ahn)
dǐpìan

Xìanzài take the *(ssee-ah)* **xīa bá gè** labels and label **zhè xīe dōngxi.** Better yet, assemble them
next (M) things *(dwong-ssee)*

(zi) *(chee-ahng-jee-ow)*
zài qíangjǐao of your **fángzi.**
in corner

Nǐ shì dōngtīan hùoshì xìatīan **qù Zhōnggúo lǚxíng?** Do not **wàng . . .**
(dwong-tee-ahn) winter *(ssee-ah-tee-ahn)* summer *(chee-oo)* go *(wahng)* forget

(yoh-yong-yee)
yóuyǒngyī
swimsuit

(lee-ahng-ssee-eh)
líangxíe
sandals

(yeh)
Yě do not forget the basic toiletries!
also

(fay-zow)
féizào

féizào ✓

(yah-shwah)
yáshūa

(yah-gow)
yágāo

(gwah-lee-ahn-dow)
gūalǐandāo

(choo-hahn-jee)
chúhànjī
deodorant

(shoo-zuh)
shūzi

For the rest of the **dōngxi,** let's start with the outside layers and work our way in.

(wi-yee)
wàiyī _____ ✓

(yoo-yee)
yǔyī _____ ☐

(sahn)
sǎn _____ ☐

(shoh-tow)
shǒutào _____ ☐

(mow-zuh)
màozi _____ ☐

(ssee-yoo-eh-zuh)
xuēzi _____ ☐

(ssee-eh)
xīe _____ ☐

(wah-zuh)
wàzi _____ ☐

(koo-wah)
kùwà _____ ☐

Take the **xìa** *(ssee-ah)* **shíwu** *(shr-woo)* **gè** labels and label **zhè xīe dōngxi.** *(dwong-ssee)* Check and make sure that **tāmén**
next   fifteen (M)   things

are clean and ready for **nǐde lǚxíng.** Be sure to do the same with the rest of the

dōngxi nǐ pack. Check them off on this list as **nǐ** organize them. **Cóng xiànzài** *(tswong)* on, **nǐ**
                                                                        from now

yǒu "feīzào" *(yoh)* *(fay-zow)* and not "soap."
have

(shwee-yee)
shùiyī _____ ☐

(shwee-pow)
shùipào _____ ☐

(twoh-ssee-eh)
tūoxíe _____ ☐

(shwee-pow) *(twoh-ssee-eh)*
Shùipáo hé tūoxíe can double for **nǐ** at the **yóuyǒng** *(yoh-yong)* **chí.** *(chr)*
bathrobe   slippers   swimming   pool

102

(ssee-jwahng) **xizhuang**	_____ ☐
(leeng-di) **lingdai**	_____ ☐
(shoh-jwahn) **shoujuan**	_____ ☐
(chun-yee) **chènyi**	_chènyī_ ☐
(shahng-yee) **shàngyi**	_____ ☐
(koo-zuh) **kùzi**	_____ ✓
(chahng-yee-foo) **chángyifu**	_____ ☐
(chun-yee) **chènyi**	_____ ☐
(choon-zuh) **qúnzi**	_____ ☐
(mow-yee) **máoyi**	_____ ☐
(ssee-wong-jow) **xiongzhǎo**	_____ ☐
(chun-choon) **chènqún**	_____ ☐
(nay-koo) **nèikù**	_____ ☐
(nay-yee) **nèiyi**	_____ ☐

Having assembled **zhè dōngxi, nǐ** are ready for **nǐde lǚxíng**. However, being human means occasionally forgetting something. Look again at the (bi-hwoh) (dee-ahn-duh) **bǎihòu dìande** directory.
department store's

Zài (jee) **jǐ** (loh) **lóu** will **nǐ** find . . .
which floor

(nahn-ruhn-duh) **nánrénde** (yee-foo) **yifú?** men's clothing	**Zài** _____ (loh) **lóu.** floor	
(new-ruhn-duh) **nǚrénde** (mow-zuh) **màozi?** women's hats	**Zài** _____ **lóu.**	
shū?	**Zài** _____ **lóu.**	
nǚrénde (nay-yee) **nèiyi** underwear	**Zài** _____ **lóu.**	

103

(ssee-eh)
xíe?
shoes

Zài _____ lóu.
floor

(wah-zuh)
wàzi?
socks

Zài _____ lóu.
floor

nǔrénde yīfú? *(yee-foo)*
clothing

Zài _____ lóu.
floor

Xìanzai just remember your basic **wèntí.** Repeat the **dǐanxíngde** *(dee-ahn-sseeng-duh)* **dùihùa** *(dwee-hwah)* below out loud
typical   conversation

and repeat it again by filling in the blanks.

Nǎr yǒu nǔrénde kùzi? *(koo-zuh)* _____
trousers

Zài nǔrén bù. *(boo)* _____
department

Nǔrén bù zài nǎr? *(boo)*   *nǔrén bù zài nǎr?*
department

Zài èr lóu. *(loh)* _____
floor

Zài nǎr mǎi yágāo? *(yah-gow)* _____
toothpaste

Zài yī lóu. _____

Nǐ búyào *(boo-yow)* **wàng le** *(wahng)* **wèn . . .** *(wuhn)*
don't   forget   to ask

Dìantī zài nǎr? *(dee-ahn-tee)* _____
elevator

Lóutī zài nǎr? *(loh-tee)* _____
stairs

Zìdòng dìantī zài nǎr? *(zuh-dwong) (dee-ahn-tee)* _____
escalator

Whether **nǐ xūyào** *(ssee-oo-yow)* **yì tíao** *(tee-ow)* **nǔrénde kùzi** *(koo-zuh)* **hùoshì yì jian** *(jee-ahn)* **nánrénde chènyī,** *(chun-yee)* the necessary **zì**
need   (M)   trousers   (M)   shirt

for shopping **shì** *(shr)* the same.
will be

(shun-muh) (chee-tsoon)
Shénme chǐcùn?
what   measurement

_____

(shr-huh)
Shìhe.
it fits

Shìhé.

_____

(boo-shr-huh)
Búshìhe.
it does not fit

_____

(yee-foo) (chee-tsoon)
Yīfú Chǐcùn: NǓRÉN
clothing   measurements

(ssee-eh) xie shoes									
Měiguo	5	5 ½	6	6 ½	7	7 ½	8	8 ½	9
Zhōngguo	35	35	36	37	38	38	38	39	40

(yee-foo) yīfú — clothing

Měiguo	8	10	12	14	16	18
Zhōngguo	36	38	40	42	44	46

(chun-yee) (mow-yee) chènyī, máoyī — blouses, sweaters

Měiguo	32	34	36	38	40	42	44
Zhōngguo	40	42	44	46	48	50	52

(ssee-ahng) (yow)
Wǒ xiǎng yào zhè gè.
     this (M)

_____

(dwoh-show) (chee-ahn)
Nà gè dūoshǎo qian?
   how much   money

_____

(yee-goong) (ssee-eh-ssee-eh)
Yīgong dūoshǎo? Xiexie.
altogether   how much   thank you

_____

Yīfú Chǐcùn: NÁNRÉN
measurements

xie										
Měiguo	7	7 ½	8	8 ½	9	9 ½	10	10 ½	11	11 ½
Zhōngguo	39	40	41	42	43	43	44	44	45	45

Yīfú								
Měiguo	34	36	38	40	42	44	46	48
Zhōngguo	44	46	48	50	52	54	56	58

chènyī, máoyī shirts								
Měiguo	14	14 ½	15	15 ½	16	16 ½	17	17 ½
Zhōngguo	36	37	38	39	40	41	42	43

Xìanzài, nǐ are **(yoo-bay) yūbèi (how) hǎo le** for your **lǚxíng.** The next Step will give nǐ a quick
     prepared   well

introduction to **Zhōngguo** signs and then nǐ are off to the **(fay-jee-chahng) fēijīchǎng.** **(yee) (loo) (peeng) (ahn) Yī lǜ píng ǎn!**
    airport   safe and peaceful journey

Step 23

 = **Caution**

Zhèr shì some of the most important **Zhōngguó** signs.
(ssee-ow) (sseen)
Xǐao xīn!
be careful

Yǐ lù píng ān!
safe and peaceful journey

Hot

Cold

Push

Pull

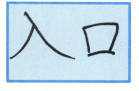

Entrance

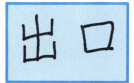

Exit

No entrance

Vacant

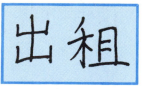

For hire; for rent

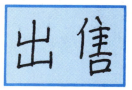

For sale

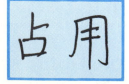

Occupied

客满

Sold out

已预定

Reserved

售票处

Ticket office

出纳

Cashier

大减价

Sales

禁止摄影

No photos allowed

危险

Danger

停止

Stop

禁止游泳

No bathing

请勿触摸

Do not touch

电梯

Elevator

关闭

Closed

请按铃

Please ring

GLOSSARY

A

ǎi	short
āsìpǐlín	aspirin

B

bā	eight
bǎ	(M)
bái	white
bǎi	one hundred
bǎihùo	things
bǎihùo dìan	department store
báitian	daytime
bàn	half
bàng	pound, pounds
bàngōngshì	office
báo	thin
bāogǔo	parcel
bàozhǐ	newspaper
bāshí	eighty
báyùe	August
bēi	glass, cup
běi	north
bèi	quilt
běibianr	the north
běifāng	northern
Běijīng	Peking
běn	bound together (M)
běndì dìanhùa	local telephone call
bǐ	writing instrument
bianr	side
biao	watch
biaogé	form, schedule
bìng	ice
bìng	sick
bìng dǐan	freezing point
bīngxiang	refrigerator
bōlí, bōlíbēi	glass
bówùgǔan	museum
bù	department
bù	not
bùhǎo, bù hǎo	not good, bad
búshìhé	it does not fit

C

cài	dishes
cài	vegetable
cài dìan	vegetable store
càichǎng	market
càidǎn	menu
cáiféng dìan	tailor's
canchē	dining car
cānjin	napkin
cǎo	grass
cèsǔo	lavatory
chá	tea
chà	before, lacking
chà yí kè	one quarter before
chá bēi	teacup
chàbùdūo	about
chágǔan	teahouse
cháng	long
cháng, chángcháng	often
chàngpìan	records
chángtú dìanhùa	long-distance telephone call
chángyīfú	dress

chángzi	sausage
chǎo	stir-fried
chápìaoyúan	conductor
chāzi	fork
chē	vehicle, car
chē zhàn	(vehicle) stop
chēfáng	garage
chéngshì	city
chènqun	underslip
chènyī	shirt, blouse
chēxiang	compartment
chí	pool
chī	to eat
chǐcùn	measurement
chīfàn	to eat meal
chízi	spoon
chōuyān	smoke
chū	out
chúan	boat
chúang	bed
chūanghù	window
chūanglían	curtain
chūzuchē	taxi
chúfáng	kitchen
chúhànjì	deodorant
chūkǒu	exit
chūntian	spring
cíqì	porcelain
cóng	from

D

dà	big
dǎ	to make (telephone call, telegram)
dǎ	to travel/by
dàdào	boulevard
dài	to bring
dǎkāi	to open
dàlù	mainland
dàn	egg
dānchéng	one-way
dānzi	slip
dào	to, arrive
dāozi	knife
dàxiao	size
Dégúo	Germany
dēng	light
Déwén	German
dī	low
dian	o'clock
dìan	store, shop
dìan	electricity
dìanbào	telegram
dìanchē	trolley
dìanhùa	telephone, telephone call
dìanhùa bù	telephone book
dìanhùa tíng	telephone booth
dianxin lèi	snack
dìanqì pin	electrical goods
dìanshì	television
dìanxíng	typical
dìanyǐng	movie
dìanyǐngyúan	movie theater
dìbā	eighth
dìfang	place
dìng	to book, reserve
dǐpìan	film
dìqī	seventh
dìshàng	floor
dìtǎn	carpet

dìtú	map
dǐu	to lose
dìxìahì	basement
dìxìatiedàochē	subway
dǒng	to understand
dōng	east
dōngbianr	the east
dòngcí	verb, verbs
dōngfāng	eastern, oriental
dōngfāng hùo	oriental goods
dōngtian	winter
dòngwùyúan	zoo
dōngxi	thing, things
dōngyáng	East Ocean, Japan
dòu	all
dòu	bean
dù	degrees
dǔan	short
dùibùqǐ	excuse me
dùihùa	conversation, conversations
dùihùan chù	money-exchange office
dūo	many, much
dūoshǎo	how much?

E

è	hungry
èr	two
èr děng	second-class
èr hūn pù	delicatessen
èrshí	twenty
èryùe	February
érzi	son

F

Fǎgúo	France
fàn	meal
fàn	rice
fáng	room
fangfǎ	ways
fángjīan	room
fàngǔar	restaurant
fángzi	house
fàntǐng	dining room
Fǎwén	French
fei	to fly
feijī	airplane
feijīchǎng	airport
feijīpìao	airplane tickets
féizào	soap
fen	Chinese money
fen	minute, minutes
fen	pink
fójìao	Buddhist
fùbì	Chinese money
fùjì	remarks
fùjìn	vicinity
fùqin	father
fúwùyúan	service person

G

gǎng	steel
gāngbǐ	pen
gānxǐ	dry clean
gānxǐ dìan	dry cleaner's
gāo	tall
gàosù	to tell
gè	(M)
gēge	brother

gěi .... to give
gěi qián .... to pay
gēn .... with
gōngchǐ .... meters
gōnggòng .... public
gōnggòng diànhùa .... public telephone
gōnggòngqìchē .... bus
gōngjù .... tools
gōnglǐ .... kilometers
gōngyù .... boarding room
gōngyúan .... park
gǒu .... dog
guāfēng .... windy
guāliandāo .... razor
guǎn .... place, hall
guānmén .... to close, closed
gǔdǒng .... antiques
gǔdǒng diàn .... antique store
gūgu .... aunt
gùi .... expensive
gùitái .... counter
gùizi .... cupboard
gúo .... nation, state
gùo .... after
gùo yí kè ...... one quarter after
gǔojiàng .... jam
gúonèi .... domestic
gúowài .... international

H

hǎi .... sea
hǎibīn .... seashore
hángkōngxìn .... air mail
hǎo .... good
hào .... number
hǎo .... well
hē .... to drink
hé .... and
hēi .... black
Hélán .... Netherlands
hěn .... very
hóng .... red
hòu .... thick
hòubīanr .... behind
hòuchē shì ..... waiting room
hùa .... language
hùai .... bad
hùan (chē) .... to transfer (vehicle)
hùan le qián ... to have exchanged money
húang .... yellow
húangyóu .... butter
hùar .... picture
hùar .... flower
hùar diàn .... flower shop
húashì .... Fahrenheit
hūayúan .... garden
hùi .... gray
hùi .... concert, meeting
hùi .... can
hújīao .... pepper
hǔo .... fire, flame
hǔochē .... train
hǔochē zhàn ..... train station
hùoshì .... or
hǔotǔi .... ham
hùzhào .... passport

J

jī .... chicken
jǐ .... some
jǐ .... how many?

jīa .... home
jīa pǔ .... family system
jīajù .... furniture
jīalǐ .... home
jīalún .... gallons
jīan .... fried
jìan .... to see, to meet
jìanglùo .... to land
jìankāng .... healthy
jīao .... Chinese money
jìao ...... to be called, called
jìao .... to order
jīao .... corner
jìaotáng .... church
jìaqían .... prices
jīatíng .... family
jīayóu zhàn ..... gas station
jīdàn .... chicken eggs
jīdūjìao .... Protestant
jīe .... street
jīedào bàngōngshì ..... street, subdistict
                      office
jìn .... into, in
jīn .... golden
jìn zhǐ tōng xíng .... no trespassing
jīnglǐ .... manager
jìngzi .... mirror
jìnìanpǐn .... souvenirs
jìnìanpǐn diàn ..... souvenir store
jīntīan .... today
jìu .... only
jǐu .... wine
jǐu .... nine
jǐugǔanr .... tavern
jǐushí .... ninety
jǐuyuè .... September
júzi .... orange
júzishǔi .... orange juice

K

kāfēi .... brown, coffee
kāfēi dìan .... coffee shop
kāi .... to boil, boils
kāi .... to open, opens
kāi .... to leave, leaves
kāichē .... to drive
kāishǐ .... to start, starts
kàn .... to read
kànjìan .... to see
kǎo .... baked
kēkǒukělè .... coke
kètīng .... living room
kùai .... fast
kùaichē .... fast train
kùaizi .... chopsticks
kùang .... mineral
kùang shǔi ..... mineral water
kùwà .... pantyhose
kùzi .... trouser

L

là .... wax
lái .... to come, comes
láihúi .... round-trip
lán .... blue
lǎo .... old
lèi .... type
lěng .... cold
lěngpán ..... cold dishes (hors d'oeuvres)

lǐ .... inside
lǐang .... two
líangxíe .... sandals
lǐfà .... haircut
lǐfà dìan .... hairdresser's
líng .... zero
lǐngdài .... tie
línyù .... shower
lìshǐ .... history
lìu .... six
lìushí .... sixty
lìuyuè .... June
lóu .... floor
lù .... route
lǜ .... green
lǚgǔan .... hotel
lǚkè ..... passenger, traveler, tourist
lǚxíng .... travel
lǚxíng shè .... travel agent
lúzi .... stove

M

mǎi .... to buy, buys
mài .... to sell, sells
màipìan .... cereal
màipìaode .... ticket-seller
Mǎlì .... Mary
mǎmǎhūhū .... so-so
màn .... slow
máo .... Chinese money
māo .... cat
máo .... wool
máojīn .... towel, towels
máoyi .... sweater
màozi .... hat
mǎtǒng .... toilet
méi .... did not
méi .... coal
Měigúo .... America
Měigúorén .... American
mèimei .... sister
měishùgǔan ...... art gallery
mén .... door
ménlíng .... doorbell
mǐ .... rice
mì .... honey
mìan .... noodles
mìan gǔanr ...... noodle shop
mìanbāo .... bread
mìanbāo dìan ...... bakery
mìao .... temple
mǐao .... seconds
míngtīan .... tomorrow
míngtīan jìan ... see you tomorrow
míngtīan xìawǔ jìan .. see you tomorrow
                       afternoon
míngxìnpìan .... postcard, postcards
míngzi .... name, names
mǔqīn .... mother

N

nà .... that, those
nǎ .... which
nán .... male
nán .... south
nánbīanr .... the south
nánfāng .... southern
nánrén .... man, men
nàozhōng .... alarm clock
nǎr .... where
náshǒucài .... specialties (food)

něi	which
nèikù	underpants
nèiyī	undershirt
néng	to be able to/can
nǐ	you
Nǐ hǎo ma?	How are you?
nían	year
níanqīng	young
niao	bird
nǐde	your
nǐmén	you
Nín mànman chī	Good appetite
níu	cow
níu ròu, níuròu	beef
níunǎi	milk
níunǎi dìan	dairy
nǚ	female
nǔan	warm
nǔér	daughter
nǔrén	woman, women

O

Oūzhōu	Europe

P

pángbīanr	next to
pánzi	plate
péng yǒu	friend
piányi	inexpensive
pí	skin, leather, peel
piao	ticket, tickets
píbāo	purse
píjīazi	wallet
píjiu	beer
píng	bottle
píngcháng	usually
pínggǔo	apple
pō	slope
pǔtōngchē	ordinary train

Q

qī	seven
qí	astride
qian	thousand
qían	money
qīanbǐ	pencil
qíanbīanr	in front of
qíang	wall
qíangjīao	corner
qǐaokèlì	chocolate
qìchē	car
qín	musical instrument
qìng	fine, clear
qìng	please
qǐngwèn	may I ask
qíong	poor
qìshǔi	soda pop
qíu	ball
qīutīan	autumn
qíyùe	July
qìyóu	gasoline
qìwēn	temperature
qù	to go
qúnzi	skirt

R

rè	hot
rén	person, people

rènhé	any
rénxíngdào	sidewalk
Rìběn	Japan
rìlì	calendar
rìyòng	everyday use
Rìwén	Japanese
róngyì	easy
ròu	meat
ròu dìan	butcher's
rùkǒu	entrance

S

sālà	salad
sǎn	umbrella
sān	three
sānlúnchē	pedicab
sānshí	thirty
sānyùe	March
shāfā	sofa
shān	mountain
shàng	up
shàng	on, on top of
shàng	to climb/to get on
shàng (chē)	to board (vehicle)
shàngbīanr	over, above
shāngdìan	store
shàngwǔ	morning
shàngyī	jacket
shǎo	little
shāo	roasted
shéi	who
shénme	what
shénme shíhòu	when, what time
shēng	voice
shèshì	Centigrade
shí	ten
shì	to be, is, are
shí	to eat
shí	stone, rock
shíbā	eighteen
shíèr	twelve
shíèryùe	December
shìhé	it fits
shíhòu	time
shíjīan bǐao	time schedule
shíjiu	nineteen
shílìu	sixteen
shípǐn dìan	grocery store
shíqī	seventeen
shísān	thirteen
shísì	fourteen
shítáng	dining room
shíwǔ	fifteen
shìwùzhāolǐng	lost-and-found office
shíyīyùe	November
shíyùe	October
shǒujùan	handkerchief
shǒujù	receipt
shòupìao chù	ticket office
shǒutào	gloves
shǒuyīnjī	radio
shū	book
shú cài	cooked vegetables
shūazi	brush
shūdìan	bookstore
shūfáng	study, den
shǔi	water
shùi	to sleep
shǔigǔo	fresh fruit
shǔigǔo dìan	fruit store

shùipáo	bathrobe
shùiyī	pajamas
shūo	to say, to speak
shūohùa	speak
shú shí	cold cuts
shūshu	uncle
shūzhūo	desk
shùzì	number, numbers
shūzi	comb
sì	four
sìjī	driver
sìshí	forty
sìyùe	April
sòng	to send
sùi	age (M)
sǔo	(M)

T

tā	he, she, it, him, her
tāde	his
táiděng	lamp
tàipíng mén	emergency gate
tàiyáng	sun
tāmén	they, them
tāng lèi	soup, soups
tāngchí	soup spoon
tánggǔo	candy
tǎngyǐ	reclining car
táoqì	ceramics
tèbíe	special
tèkùai	express train
tīan	day, days
tían	sweet
tían dǐanlèi	dessert
tīanhūabǎn	ceiling
tīanqì	weather
tīantīan	everyday
tīanzhǔjīao	Catholic
tíao	(M)
tǐeguǐ	track
tíng	booth
tíngchē	to park
tíngchē chǎng	parking lot
tínglíu	to stay
tīngtǒng	receiver
tǐwēn	body temperature
tǐyùgǔan	gymnasium
tóngzhì	comrade

W

wàigúo	foreign
wàiyī	coat
wǎn	late
wǎnfàn	dinner
wàng	toward, to
wàng	to forget
wàng chūkǒu	to the exit
wǎnshàng	evening
wǎnshàng jìan	see you in the evening
wánjù	toys
wàzi	socks
wèi	hello
wèishénme	why
wēn	warm
wén	written language
wèn	to ask
wénjù	stationery
wénjù dìan	stationery store
wèntí	question, questions

wǒ	I, me
wǒ shì	I am
wǒ zài	I am (in, at)
wǒde	my
wòfáng	bedroom
wǒmén	we
wòpù	sleeping car
wǔ	five
wǔfàn	dinner
wǔshí	fifty
wǔyuè	May
wūzi	room

X

xǐ	to wash
xī	west
xìa	next
xìa	down
xìa (chē)	to disembark
xìabianr	under, below
xìan	line
Xiao xīn!	Be careful!
xiàng	elephant
xiǎng yào	would like
xiāngjiao	banana
xiāngshǔi	perfume
xìanzài	now
xiāngzi	trunk, suitcase
xiǎo	small
xiǎohár	child, children
xiǎo máojīn	hand towel
xìatian	summer
xìawù	foggy
xìawǔ	afternoon
xìaxǔe	snows
xiayù	rains
xībianr	the west
Xībǎnyá	Spain
xǐe	several
xíe	shoes
xǐe	to write
xǐe chū	to write out
xìexie	thank you
xīfáng	western
xǐhuan	to like
xǐliǎn máojīn	washcloth
xǐliánpén	washbasin
xīn	new
xìn	letter, letters
xínglǐ	luggage
xīngqī	week
xīngqìèr	Tuesday
xīngqìlìu	Saturday
xīngqìsān	Wednesday
xīngqìsì	Thursday
xīngqìtian	Sunday
xīngqìwǔ	Friday
xīngqìyī	Monday
xīnxian	fresh
xiongzhào	brassiere
xìpìao	theater tickets
xīyáng	West Ocean, a western country
xǐyī dìan	laundry
xìyùan	theater
xǐzǎo	to bathe
xǐzǎo máojīn	bath towel
xǐzǎofáng	bathroom
xīzhuāng	suit
xúexí	to learn
xūyào	to need
xūezi	boots

Y

yā	duck
yágāo	toothpaste
yān	tobacco
yán	salt
yān dìan	tobacco store
yán shǔi	salt water
yàng	kind, type
yǎnjìng	glasses
yánsè	color, colors
yào	costs
yào	want, must
yào	to take (time)
yàochí	keys
yào dìan	pharmacy
yàofáng	pharmacy
yáshūa	toothbrush
yè	page, pages
yè, yèlǐ	night
yě	also
yī	one
yī, yīfú	clothing
yǐ, yǐzi	chair
yí kè	one quarter
Yí lù píng ān!	safe and peaceful journey
yìbǎi	one hundred
yīchú	clothes closet
Yìdàlì	Italy
yìdǐar	a little
yígòng	altogether
yǐhòu	later
yìngbì	coins
yìnggāi	to have to/should
Yīngguó	England
Yīngwén	English
yínháng	bank
yǐnliao	beverages
yínqì	silver
yīnyùe	music
yìqian	one thousand
yǐqían	before
yīshēng	doctor
yǒuyìsi	interesting
yíyàng	same
yīyùan	hospital
yíyùe	January
yìzhí zǒu	straight ahead
yòngpǐn	goods
yǒu	to have, has; there is, there are
yòu	right
Yǒu rén shūohuà	the line is busy
yòubianr	right, right side
yóujìan	mail
yóujú	post office
yóupìao	stamp
yǒuqían	rich
yǒurén	occupied
yóutǒng	mailbox
yóuyǒng chí	swimming pool
yóuyǒngyī	swimsuit
yóuzhèng	postal
yú	fish
yú dìan	fish store
yúan	unit of Chinese currency
yùe	month, months
yūehàn	John
yùetái	platform
yún	cloud
yǔxīa lèi	seafood

yuyī	raincoat

Z

zá	mixed
záhùo	miscellaneous goods
záhùo dìan	drugstore
zài	is (in, at); are (in, at)
zài	again
zài jìan	see you again
zài shūo	repeat
zǎofàn	breakfast
zázhì	magazine
zěnme	how
zhá	fried
zhàn	stop, station
zhàn	to stand
zhǎng	(M)
zhàng	account
zhàngdān	bill
zhǎnlǎnguǎn	exhibition hall
zhǎo	to look for
zhàopìan	photo
zhàoxìang qìcái dìan	camera store
zhàoxìangjī	camera
zhè, zhèi	this, these
zhēng	steamed
zhèngcháng	normal
zhèngqùe	correct
zhěntóu	pillow
zhèr	here
zhǐ	only
zhǐ	paper
zhǐbì	currency
zhīdào	to know
zhōng	clock
zhōngbiao	clocks, watches
zhōngbiao dìan	watchmaker's
Zhōngguó	China
zhōngjīan	middle
Zhōngwén	Chinese
zhōngyāng	central
zhōngyāng gōngyúan	central park
zhōngtóu	hour, hours
zhòngyào	important
zhǔ	boiled
zhù	to live, to reside
zhǔan	to turn
zhǔan jǐao	around the corner
zhùangyán	magnificent
zhūozi	table
zhūròu, zhū ròu	pork
zì	word, words
zì dǐan	dictionary
zìdòng dìantī	escalator
zìxíng chē	bicycle
zìzhǐlǒu	wastepaper basket
zōngjìao	religion, religions
zǒngzhàn	main station
zǒu	to walk
zǒu jìn	to enter
zǔfù	grandfather
zǔfùmǔ	grandparents
zǔmǔ	grandmother
zùo	to do, to make
zǔo	left
zùo	(M)
zùo	by
zùo	to sit
zǔobianr	left, left side
zúotian	yesterday
zùowèi	seat

111

DRINKING GUIDE

This drinking guide is intended to explain the sometimes overwhelming variety of beverages available to you while in China. It is by no means complete. Some of the experimenting has been left up to you, but this should get you started. The asterisks (*) indicate brand names.

CHÁ (tea)

hóng chá	black tea
chímén hóng chá	
lìchēe hóng chá	
lǜ chá	green tea
xiangpìan	jasmine tea
wǔlóng chá	fermented tea
qīng chá	plain tea

LÌEJǏU (spirits)

báilándì	brandy
wēishìjì	whiskey
lúomùjǐu	rum
wǒdékǎ	vodka

JǏU (wine)

pútáojǐu	grape wine
hóng pútáojǐu	red wine
bǎi pútáojǐu	white wine
zhúyèqīng	white wine
lǜdào shāojǐu	very strong white wine
máotáijǐu	white wine (from Guizhou Province)
fēnjǐu	white wine (from Shanxi Province)
gāolíangjǐu	sorghum wine
húang jǐu	rice wine (from Shaoxing Province)
xiāngbīn	champagne

PÍJǏU (beer)

*Qīngtǎo
*Hǎiōu

QÍTǍ YǏNLÌAO (other drinks)

kěkǒukělè	cola
sūan méi tāng	soft drink made from dried prunes, sugar and spices
qì shǔi	carbonated water
kùang shǔi	mineral water
sūdá shǔi	soda water
júzishǔi	orange juice
níunǎi	milk
kāfēi	coffee
kěkě	cocoa
rè qǐaokèlì	hot chocolate

Càidān
menu

FANGUAR

Qīng cài lèi (vegetables)

dòuyá	bean sprouts
sŭn	bamboo shoots
cōng	green onions
jiāng	ginger
qíncài	celery
báicài	cabbage
bōcài	spinach
mógu	mushrooms
huáng gūa	cucumbers
biǎndòu	beans
wāndòu	peas

Shŭiguŏ (fruit)

júzi	orange
lǐzi	plum
táozi	peach
xiāngjiāo	banana
gānzi	tangerine
bíqi	water chestnuts
mángguŏ	mango
wúhuāguŏ	figs
lìzhī	litchee
yīngtáo	cherries
píngguŏ	apple
méizi	prune
pútáo	grapes
zǎozi	dates
níngméng	lemon
yángméi	strawberries
mùméi	raspberries

Diǎnxīn lèi (snacks)

dòu shā bāo	steamed bun with red-bean paste
cài bāo	steamed bun with pork and vegetables
zhī má bǐng	sesame crisp cake

Yinliao (beverages)

chá	tea
kāfēi	coffee
niúnǎi	milk
jiŭ	wine
píjiŭ	beer
júzishŭi	orange juice
kuàng shŭi	mineral water

Zuo fǎ (ways of preparation)

mìan tūo	in batter
zhŭ	boiled
kǎo	baked
shāo	roasted
zhēng	steamed
pèng	braised
zhá	fried, deep-fried
chǎo	stir-fried

Chángyòngde (general)

yán	salt
hújiao	pepper
yóu	oil
cù	vinegar
jièmò	mustard
jiang yóu	soy sauce
táng	sugar

Nín mànmān chī!

Mian fàn lèi (rice and noodles)

- bái fàn — plain rice
- dàn chǎo fàn — fried rice with egg
- jī sī miàn — noodles with shredded chicken
- ròu sī miàn — noodles with shredded pork
- xiā rén miàn — noodles with shrimp
- dōng gū miàn — noodles with mushrooms
- zhū gān miàn — noodles with pork liver
- sù cài miàn — noodles with vegetables
- chǎo miàn — fried noodles
- xiā rén chǎo miàn — fried noodles with shrimp

Lěng pán lèi (cold dishes)

- bái qiē jī — cold chicken
- wǔ xiāng yā — spicy duck
- yóu bào xiā — oil-fried shrimps
- xūn yú — smoked fish
- wǔ xiāng niúròu — spiced beef
- xián dàn — preserved egg
- yán shuǐ yā — salted duck
- bàn hǎi zhé — fish jelly
- là cài — hot, pickled mustard greens
- xián huā shēng — salted peanuts

Tāng lèi (soup)

- qīng cài dòu fu tāng — bean curd and vegetable soup
- báicài tāng — cabbage soup
- xī hóng shì dàn tāng — tomato and egg soup
- dōng guā tāng — winter melon soup
- niúròu tāng — beef soup
- xièròu tāng — crab soup
- jī tāng — chicken soup
- bèikè tāng — scallop soup
- zhā cài tāng — vegetable soup

Zhūròu lèi (pork)

- tāng cù pái gǔ — sweet-and-sour spareribs
- tāng cù lǐ jī — sweet-and-sour pork
- shīzi tóu — pork meatballs
- qīng jiāo ròu sī — pork with green pepper
- gān zhá zhū pái — fried pork fillet
- chǎo zhū gān — stir-fried pork liver
- chǎo yāo huār — stir-fried pork kidney

Niúròu lèi (beef)

- tāng cù niúròu wán — sweet-and-sour meatballs
- chǎo niúròu sī — stir-fried beef
- gān biān niúròu sī — dry-stir-fried beef
- niúròu yáng cōng — fried beef with onions
- hóng shāo niúròu — beef stew in soy sauce
- niúròu gài lán cài — fried beef with broccoli
- gā lí niúròu — curried beef

Jīya lèi (poultry)

- jī — chicken
- yā — duck
- chún — quail
- yěji — pheasant
- huǒjī — turkey
- é — goose
- gēzi — pigeon
- chǎo jī sī — fried chicken shreds
- jī sī chǎo sǔn — fried chicken with bamboo shoots
- gā lí jī — curried chicken
- kǎo yā — glazed duck

Yúxia lèi (seafood)

- tǎyú — sole
- guīyú — salmon
- guìyú — Mandarin fish
- jìyú — perch
- xuěyú — cod
- lǐyú — carp
- píngyú — turbot
- pángxie — crab
- háo — oysters
- shànbèiké — scallops
- xiā — shrimp
- lóngxiā — lobster
- dàxia — prawns
- zhá dà xiā — fried shrimp
- chǎo xiā piàn — fried, sliced prawns
- pēng dà xiā — braised prawns
- zhà yú tiáor — fried fish slices
- tāng cù yú — sweet-and-sour fish
- hóng shāo yú — sautéed fish in soy sauce
- qīng zhēng yú — steamed Mandarin fish
- tāng cù lǐ yú — sweet-and-sour Mandarin fish
- tāng cù huáng yú — sweet-and-sour yellow fish
- qīng zhēng xiè — steamed crab
- xiè fěn cài xīn — crab with vegetables
- miàn tiáo xiè — fried crab in batter
- fú róng xiè — crab with egg

- zhāng chá yā — fried duck in spices
- cuì pí yā — crispy duck

Dòu fu lèi (bean curd)

- hóng shāo dòu fu — bean curd with soy sauce
- má pó dòu fu — bean curd with pepper
- dōng gū dòu fu — bean curd with mushrooms
- xiā rén dòu fu — bean curd with shrimp

(jee-ow) **jìao**	*(li)* **lái**
(my) **mǎi**	*(chee-oo)* **qù**
(shwoh) **shūo**	*(yoh)* **yǒu**
(joo) **zhù**	*(ssee-yoo-eh-ssee)* **xúexí**
(jee-ow) **jìao**	*(ssee-ahng)* *(yow)* **xǐang yào**
(teeng-lee-oo) **tínglíu**	*(ssee-oo-yow)* **xūyào**

to come	to be called
to go	to buy
to have	to speak
to learn	to live/reside
would like	to order
to need	to stay/remain

(my)
mài

(shwoh)
shūo

(kahn-jee-ahn)
kanjìan

(chr)
chī

(swong)
sòng

(huh)
hē

(shwee)
shùi

(jahn)
zhàn

(jow)
zhǎo

(dwong)
dǒng

(dah)
dà

(zi) *(shwoh)*
zài shūo

to say	to sell
to eat	to see
to drink	to send
to stand	to sleep
to understand	to look for
to say again	to make (telephone call, telegram)

(kahn)
kàn

(ssee-eh)
xǐe

(shr)
shì

(gay)
gěi

(goong-zwoh)
gōngzùo

(gay)   *(chee-ahn)*
gěi qían

(fay)
fēi

(nung)
néng

(zwoh)
zùo

(yeeng-gi)
yīnggāi

(shwoh-shr)
shōushí

(juhr-dow)
zhīdaò

to write	to read
to give	to be
to pay	to work
to be able to/can	to fly
to have to/should	to sit
to know	to pack

(zoh) **zǒu**	*(ki-shr)* **kāishǐ**
(zoh) *(jeen)* **zǒu jìn**	*(ki)* **kāi**
(ssee-ah) *(chuh)* **xìa chē**	*(zwoh-fahn)* **zùofàn**
(shahng) *(chuh)* **shàng chē**	*(jee-ahng-lwoh)* **jìanglùo**
(hwahn) *(chuh)* **hùan chē**	*(deeng)* **dìng**
(dow) **dào**	*(yow)* *(chee-ahn)* **yào _____ qían** *(?)*

to start	to walk
to open	to enter
to cook	to disembark
to land	to board
to reserve	to transfer
to cost	to arrive

(gwahn)
gūan

(ki)
kāi

(ssee)
xǐ

(lew-sseeng)
lǚxíng

(jee-ow-hwahn)
jīaohuàn

(choh-yahn)
chōuyān

(dee-oo)
dīu

(wuhn)
wèn

(woh) *(shr)*
wǒ shì

(ssee-ah-ssee-yoo-eh) *(luh)*
Xìaxǔe le.

(woh-muhn) *(shr)*
wǒmén shì

(ssee-ah-yoo) *(luh)*
Xìayǔ le.

to depart	to close
to travel	to wash
to smoke	to exchange
to ask	to lose
It is snowing.	I am
It is raining.	we are

(gow) *(dee)* **gāo - dī**	*(tah)* *(shr)* **tā shì**
(chee-wong) *(yoh-chee-ahn)* **qíong - yǒuqían**	*(nee)* *(shr)* **nǐ shì**
(dwahn) *(chahng)* **dǔan - cháng**	*(tah-muhn)* *(shr)* **tāmén shì**
(beeng) *(jee-ahn-keeng)* **bìng - jìankāng**	*(zi)* *(jee-ahn)* **Zài jìan.**
(pee-ahn-yee) *(gwee)* **píanyì - gùi**	*(nuhr)* *(yoh)* **nèr yǒu**
(low) *(nee-ahn-cheeng)* **lǎo - níanqīng**	*(nee)* *(how)* *(mah)* **Nǐ hǎo ma?**

he
she } is   high - low
it

you are   poor - rich

they are   short - long

See you again.   sick - healthy

there is/there are   cheap - expensive

How are you?   old - young

(kwy) **kùai** - *(mahn)* **màn**	*(how)* **hǎo** - *(hwy)* **hùai**
(hoh) **hòu** - *(bow)* **báo**	*(roo-ahn)* **rǔan** - *(yeeng)* **yìng**
(dwoh) **dūo** - *(show)* **shǎo**	*(gow)* **gāo** - *(i)* **ǎi**
(roo-koh) **rùkǒu** - *(choo-koh)* **chūkǒu**	*(ruh)* **rè** - *(lung)* **lěng**
(tee-ahn) **tían** - *(swahn)* **sūan**	*(zwoh)* **zǔo** - *(yoh)* **yòu**
(dwee-boo-chee) **dùibùqǐ**	*(shahng)* **shàng** - *(ssee-ah)* **xìa**

good - bad	fast - slow
soft - hard	thick - thin
tall - short	a lot - a little
hot - cold	entrance - exit
left - right	sweet - sour
above - below	excuse me